GEOGRAPHY FIELDWORK

Ⓜ Macmillan Education

First published 1986
Reprinted 1987

Published by
MACMILLAN EDUCATION LTD
Houndmills, Basingstoke, Hampshire RG21 2XS
and London
Companies and representatives
throughout the world

Designed by Wendy Bann
Cover photograph: Jim Turner

Printed in Hong Kong

Frew, Jennifer
Geography Fieldwork
1. Geography—Field work
I. Title
910′.724   G74.5

ISBN 0-333-37689-7

CONTENTS

INTRODUCTION

IMPORTANT
Read these pages first

In a field study, you are undertaking your own research work. It is like being an explorer or a detective. You are investigating some part of the world which may never have been looked at in this way before.

Geographers, explorers and detectives work in an organised way:

An explorer
1. wants to *examine* a new area, but not until

2. he has kept a detailed and accurate *field record* of his observations, and

3. then *assessed* his recordings,

4. can he *draw conclusions* to make a worthwhile report.

A detective
1. has his own *suspicions about a case* he must investigate, but

2. he must first *collect and record* accurately the evidence and

3. then *sift* it all before

4. he can say if he has *proved his case.*

Similarly, field study in geography falls into four main sections:
1. **purpose of investigation**: you must have an aim behind your work and this will influence your
2. **methods of investigations** and **recording in the field**; then you must
3. **process the information you have collected** to reach

4. **conclusions** about your first aims.

Your aim may be to make a detailed investigation like an explorer, and to present your discoveries in an organised way. If, like a detective, you suspect that a certain pattern exists in your fieldwork area this is your hypothesis and your aim is to prove it: this is called **testing a hypothesis**.

Each chapter in this book has an introduction to its topics to help you to choose the one you find most interesting. Your teacher will help you to choose the investigation best suited to you and to your fieldwork area. You should then work carefully through it step by step until you reach a conclusion.

Each investigation may be undertaken on an individual, group or class basis, and the work is structured to enable the fieldwork to be completed within a few hours locally or as part of a few days of fieldwork away from home.

The format of each investigation is intended to enable you to use your time both in the field and in school efficiently and with the minimum of supervision. Each investigation consists of five parts:
an introduction to the topic;
preparation and planning, including the making of equipment where appropriate;
fieldwork methods;
follow-up work including data processing;
the drawing of conclusions.

Detailed observation and recording (exploring) may be

combined with, or kept distinct from the hypothesis-testing (detective) approach.

The equipment suggested in this book is, wherever possible, home-made. Although it is desirable to use precision instruments the high cost of these often makes their use unlikely. You may well notice this most in the chapter on weather.

All the questionnaires and lists may be produced inexpensively and quickly by using the program given in the Appendix. An example of a questionnaire produced in this way is in 'Weather' on page 80. After the initial work a copy of the item should be stored on cassette or disc for further reproduction. A microcomputer will enable results from a group to be collated and tabulated easily and accurately.

EQUIPMENT FOR FIELDWORK

Before you begin your fieldwork always check that you have every item in the **basic fieldkit**.

**SAFETY IS MOST
IMPORTANT
OF ALL
Tell your teacher and
parents
where you are going and
when you expect to return.
Do not take risks.
Follow the country code if
you are in open countryside.**

THE COUNTRY CODE

Guard against all risks of fire

Fasten all gates

Keep dogs under proper control

Keep to the paths across farmland

Avoid damaging fences, hedges and walls

Leave no litter

Safeguard water supplies

Protect wildlife, wild plants and trees

Go carefully on country roads

Respect the life of the countryside

BASIC FIELDKIT

1 Footwear and clothing comfortable and suitable for the weather conditions and the environment you will be working in.
2 Field notebook, bulldog paper clip, pencil and polythene bag big enough to put over your field notebook and write in if it rains.
3 A base-map of your fieldwork area. Instructions on how to draw this are given below. You may have to bring the map up to date in your fieldwork by adding new buildings and divisions of land, and by crossing out those which are no longer there. A suitable scale of map is recommended in each chapter under the heading 'Equipment'.
4 Your aims written in the front of your field notebook. Suggestions are given at the beginning of each investigation.
5 Timetable for the public transport you may use.
6 Money for public transport. Also the correct coins for use in a public telephone together with the telephone number you would ring if you needed help.
7 Your camera if you intend to use it.
8 A whistle, torch and compass for use in emergency in open countryside.

HOW TO DRAW A BASE-MAP

Trace your fieldwork area from a large scale Ordnance Survey map in your school, public library or Council Offices. Choosing the scale is very important, for example, the 1:2500 map is ideal for a very detailed study such as the use of buildings or a beach, but if you investigate, for example, the area from which people come to shop, or a large leisure area, the 1:250 000 scale will probably be big enough. Alternatively, you can draw your own as described on the next page.

HOW TO ENLARGE A MAP ACCURATELY

Choose the number of grid squares on the Ordnance Survey map which you wish to enlarge. Lay a piece of tracing paper over the squares. Use your ruler and pencil to make a grid of small squares with evenly spaced lines. Measure the distance between two of your pencil lines, and then decide how many times wider apart you want them to be on your enlarged map. Draw another larger grid of pencil lines on plain paper. Now copy the detail square by square from the printed map onto your enlarged map. Draw the details in pencil first and then in black ink or fibre-tipped pen. Finally rub out the pencil lines. Figure 1 shows an example.

Always put the north point beside your map like this

and add the scale as both the **representative fraction** (R.F.), e.g. 1:50 000, which means that everything on the ground is 50 000 times bigger than it is on your map; and as a **linear scale**:

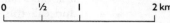

Both of these ways of showing the scale are given on all Ordnance Survey maps.

HOW TO USE YOUR CAMERA IN YOUR FIELDWORK

Buy either a black and white or colour *print* film: not slides.

When you take your photograph hold your camera so that *the object* you want to take *fills the viewfinder*.

Make sure your photograph includes *a scale* such as people, a ruler, pencil or penknife.

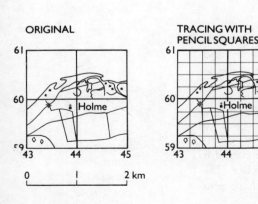

ORIGINAL

Scale: R.F. = 1:50 000

TRACING WITH
PENCIL SQUARES

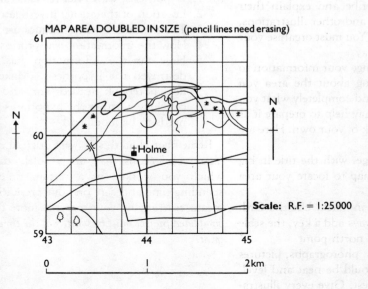

MAP AREA DOUBLED IN SIZE (pencil lines need erasing)

Scale: R.F. = 1:25 000

Figure 1

REQUESTING INFORMATION

The local public library will be able to help you with information such as:

maps of the solid geology, and drift geology,
historical maps and photographs,
planning information.

Also, they will provide the names and addresses of the secretaries of the Local History Society, Chamber of Commerce, Conservationists, etc.

Always be polite in your requests and explain why you want the information. If you write a letter, remember to enclose a stamped envelope addressed to yourself.

PRESENTING YOUR COMPLETED FIELDWORK PROJECT

Geographers, explorers and detectives cannot allow their own personal likes and dislikes to show in their conclusions. Think how very carefully explorers or detectives would have to describe and explain their findings, using maps, diagrams and other illustrations, before you would believe them. You must organise your findings in the same detailed way.

Think how you can best arrange your information so that someone, knowing nothing about the area you have investigated, can understand completely what you have discovered or proved. It may help to prepare it as if you were going to write a book of your own. Here are some hints:

(a) Make an attractive **title page**, with the title in big letters and also include a map to locate your area and/or coloured pictures.

(b) Draw **outline maps** clearly in black. Use the Ordnance Survey's symbols; always add a key, the scale and a compass to show the north point.

(c) On all **illustrations** – maps, photographs, pictures and diagrams – printing should be neat and level. Block capitals may be clearest. Give every illustra-

tion a heading and a number: Figure 1, Figure 2, and so on. Refer to these numbers in your written sections.

(d) If you have used books, or maps or photographs in a library, make a list of these in alphabetical order and call this your **bibliography**. Add this at the end of your project.

(e) Begin with a table of **contents**.

You may decide to write in detail and illustrate your fieldwork just as an explorer would do and list (a) gives suggested sections for your contents. If you have worked like a detective your contents will be similar to list (b).

(a) 1. Purpose of the investigation
    2. Location of the area(s) investigated
    3. The methods and techniques used
    4. How the information was processed
    5. Conclusions

(b) 1. Hypothesis, with brief reasons for choosing it
    2. Location of the area(s) investigated
    3. The methods and techniques used
    4. How the information was processed
    5. How far the information has supported or destroyed the hypothesis. (Make lists in your field notebook headed 'For' and 'Against' and conclude whether the hypothesis is true, false or needs to be modified.)

Remember that this is *your* original research work. Your conclusions may apply solely to the areas in which you worked at a certain time. It is worth spending time and care on your presentation even if it means rearranging your material more than once. *The completed project must be worthy of the time you have spent on it.*

OUTDOOR LEISURE AREA

What do we mean when we talk about leisure activities? Make a list of *outdoor* leisure activities, and note beside each where you would be able to pursue it near your school or home.

Outdoor leisure areas come in all shapes and sizes:

SMALL AND LOCAL Parks in urban areas, country parks, zoos, the Forestry Commission's forest trails, homes and places of historic interest belonging to the National Trust or in private ownership, sailing clubs, areas belonging to the Wildfowl Trust or to the Royal Society for the Protection of Birds, angling areas.

BIG and of NATIONAL IMPORTANCE National Parks, holiday resorts.

Recreation areas may be administered by the local authority, and an area as big as a National Park usually falls within the boundaries of several local authority areas. Can you understand some of the conflict between the interests of such people as farmers, Water Boards, Forestry Commission, protectors of wildlife and Tourist Boards? Look at your list and put a note beside those activities which you feel could be a nuisance to some groups of people such as those mentioned above.

In any leisure area the facilities provide for either **formal, organised activities** such as tennis, golf, water skiing, often needing equipment and rules, and **informal activities** such as walking, picnicking, sunbathing, photography. Some activities such as sailing and bird watching can be done either on an informal basis or more formally through a club as illustrated in the Venn Diagram in Figure 2.

Make a Venn Diagram from your own list of activities.

Before beginning fieldwork for any of the investigations in this chapter, find out as much as possible about the facilities that are available in the area that you choose to investigate. The Second Series of the 1:50 000 scale Ordnance Survey map gives tourist information.

Figure 2 Venn diagram to show some outdoor leisure activities

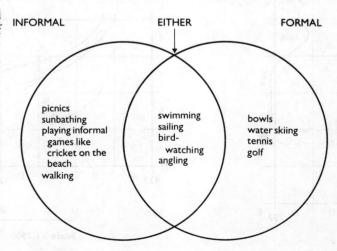

INFORMAL   EITHER   FORMAL

picnics
sunbathing
playing informal
games like
cricket on the
beach
walking

swimming
sailing
bird-
watching
angling

bowls
water skiing
tennis
golf

FIELDWORK AREAS

Choose an area from those listed above or a similar one of your choice. If you are working in pairs, confine your fieldwork to an area no bigger than 6 square kilometres or to a transect 4 kilometres long and 250 metres wide (1 km²).

If you are working in an urban area it would be interesting to study more than one leisure area.

1 : To assess the popularity by age-group of facilities available in the leisure area

PREPARATION

Make a list of all the types of facility you expect to find within the leisure area you intend to investigate. If any are privately owned, write to the manager or to the secretary explaining which school you are from and the purpose of your investigation, and request permission to proceed with it on a particular date and for the number of hours you expect to spend in the area.

On a large-scale Ordnance Survey map, preferably 1:2500, mark the boundary of the area or transect you intend to investigate. Divide the 100 m grid squares into 16 smaller squares each with sides representing 25 m or divide the transect into 25 m sections. This will be the base-map which you will use in your fieldwork so you may need to trace it. Make each small square easy to identify by letters and make sure that you are familiar, with some landscape feature within each square. Before you begin your fieldwork pace out 25 m by the method explained on page 39 and become familiar with how far away 25 m appears.

Figure 3 Base maps divided into workable squares for fieldwork

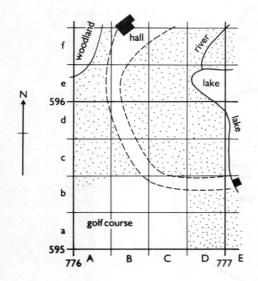

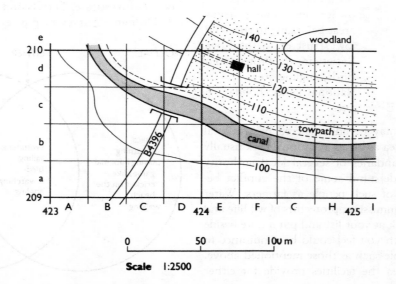

Scale 1:2500

Copy leisure information shown on the Ordnance Survey maps of 1:50 000 Second Series into each small square.

Next make a list of the facilities you expect to find within your chosen fieldwork area. Give each facility a number by which you can easily record it on your fieldwork base-map. Then make a list of the leisure pursuits, giving each a letter as shown in the example.

LIST FOR RECORDING LEISURE FACILITIES
1. Angling area (stream or lake)
2. Bowling greens
3. Café
4. Flower garden with 8 benches
5. Grassy area for informal games

LIST FOR RECORDING LEISURE PURSUITS
A Angling
B Boating
C Golfing
D Paddling
E Picnicking

Practise estimating age-groups by noticing people in bus queues, in the supermarket and in any busy place. Make sure that you can quickly place people fairly accurately into one of these age-groups:

under 10 years; 11 – 20 years; 21 – 60 years; over 60 years.

It would be ideal if you could have a third person with you during your fieldwork to record the age-group of people.

EQUIPMENT
- **Basic fieldkit**
- **Base-map divided into small squares**
- **Plain paper** divided into small squares each numbered identically to the base map.
- **List for recording leisure activities**
- **List for recording leisure pursuits**
- **4 pencils** each of different colour

FIELDWORK METHOD
One person should be in charge of recording the leisure facilities in each small square on the base-map, while the other person records in the corresponding square on the blank paper the number of people taking part in each activity.

Use your base-map as a guide to walking through the leisure area. Each time you walk into a 'new square' or 'new section' record the information which you think applies to that area. It is important to count the number of people on first sight because they may change their activity within minutes of your arrival! People playing informal cricket may decide to sit down; people in one part of the zoo may suddenly move to look at another type of animal. Estimate people's age-group and add this to your grid, going over your original stroke in the colour chosen for that age-group. Figure 4 shows an imaginary example.

Figure 4 Maps to show leisure facilities and their use

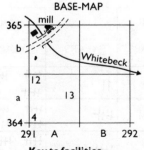

BASE-MAP

Key to facilities
4 car park
12 picnic tables
13 rides in pony and trap

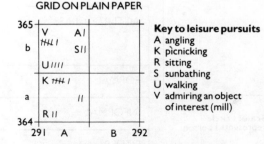

GRID ON PLAIN PAPER

Key to leisure pursuits
A angling
K pìcnicking
R sitting
S sunbathing
U walking
V admiring an object of interest (mill)

Key to age-groups
red: under 10 years
blue: 11–20 years
black: 21–60 years
yellow: over 60 years

PROCESSING THE INFORMATION

1 Sketch-map of leisure facilities

To discover whether the relief of the land has influenced the siting of any leisure facilities you will need a map with contours. Height is not represented by contours on large-scale Ordnance Survey maps, so copy these from a map of scale 1:25 000 or 1:50 000. First, trace the map used in your fieldwork and then find the grid squares covering it on the small-scale map. Divide each grid square into sixteen and number each small square for reference, as on your fieldwork map. Finally, draw the contours onto your tracing.

Work out a colour key to represent different facilities and then, referring to your fieldwork map, shade these on your traced map. Add the key.

2 Tracing overlay to show which activities were used on the fieldwork day

Place a piece of tracing paper over your shaded map, securing it by sticky tape along one edge.

Wherever a facility was being used in any way, draw in black concentric circles around a dot marked over the facility to represent the number of people using it (Figure 5). Choose the scale carefully to avoid adjacent circles overlapping: 1 circle may represent 1 person, or 1 circle may represent 5 people, and so on. Add the date and time when you made the investigation.

3 Classifying activities and calculating their area

As the Venn diagram on page 5 shows, activities may be classed as **formal**, or **informal**, but some will fit into both classes. Put the latter into a category called '**either**'. Use 'Formal', 'Informal' and 'Either' as column headings and systematically work across your map and place each activity in the appropriate column. If the activity occurs more than once place a √ beside it for each time.

Count the number in each column and illustrate it by a bar-chart. Use a different colour on the chart to represent each column.

Shade your map in the same colours to represent the area used for each facility and then, using the method described on page 96, calculate the area covered by each class of activity. Which uses the most land?

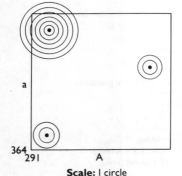

a

364
291   A

Scale: 1 circle
represents 1 person

Figure 5 How to represent the number of people using leisure facilities

ACTIVITY CLASS	UNDER 10 YEARS	11–20 YEARS	21–60 YEARS	OVER 60 YEARS	TOTAL NUMBER OF PEOPLE USING EACH ACTIVITY CLASS
FORMAL	₢卌 I	II	卌 卌 卌	III	26
INFORMAL	卌 III	卌	卌 卌 卌 IIII	卌 I	38
EITHER	IIII	卌 I	卌 卌 卌 I	II	28
TOTAL NUMBER OF PEOPLE IN EACH AGE-GROUP	18	13	50	11	92

4 Relating class of activity to age-group of users

Use your fieldwork record to complete a table like the imaginary one on page 8. Work systematically through each square or section of your investigation, ticking it off as you complete the list. The colour key and the classification you have made will ensure accuracy. Add up the total number of people in each age-group using each class of facility.

There are different ways of illustrating your fieldwork results so that they will show the relationship between age-group and the class of facility used.

(a) **Bar-chart**: Draw a bar-chart, with the number of people represented on the vertical axis and activities within each age-group represented on the horizontal axis.

(b) **Pie-chart**: Follow the instructions step by step and put your own results in place of those from page 8.

1. Draw a circle with a radius as big as possible.
2. There are 360° in a circle, so to calculate the number of degrees representing 1 person, divide 360 by the total number of people recorded: $\frac{360}{92} = 3.9°$

The number of degrees representing 1 person remains constant in all the calculations.

Multiply this number by the number of people in each class of activity in turn, and then divide the circle into three:

$$\text{formal} \quad = \frac{360}{92} \times 26 = 101.7° \text{ of the circle}$$

$$\text{informal} = \frac{360}{92} \times 38 = 148.7° \text{ of the circle}$$

$$\text{either} \quad = \frac{360}{92} \times 28 = 109.6° \text{ of the circle}$$

Draw a thick black line on the circle between each section and label the 'activity class' outside the circle.

3. Divide each 'activity class' section into four to show the number of people of each age-group using it. Calculate each in the way shown for 'formal':

$$\text{under 10 years} = \frac{360}{92} \times 6 = 23.5°$$

$$\text{11 – 20 years} \quad = \frac{360}{92} \times 2 = 7.8°$$

$$\text{21 – 60 years} \quad = \frac{360}{92} \times 15 = 58.7°$$

$$\text{over 60 years} \quad = \frac{360}{92} \times 3 = 11.7°$$

Shade each small section in the colour used for recording in the field. Add the colour key to the chart.

(c) **Proportional circles**: These are very easy to read but involve more calculation (see pages 61–2).

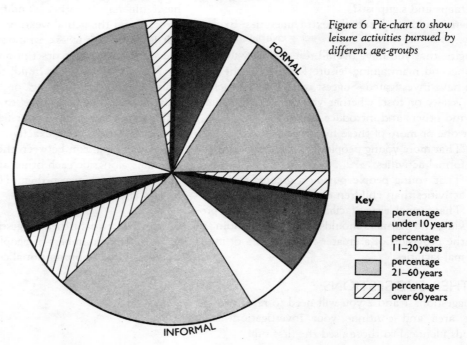

Figure 6 Pie-chart to show leisure activities pursued by different age-groups

Key

■ percentage under 10 years

□ percentage 11–20 years

▨ percentage 21–60 years

▨ percentage over 60 years

DRAWING CONCLUSIONS

1 Describe what you have discovered about the facilities available in the leisure area and how much each was used on......... (fieldwork date). Use your maps and diagrams as proof and illustration.

2 Taking each age-group in turn, describe which activities you discovered to be most popular. Suggest reasons for this.

3 Suggest ways in which you could plan to provide more facilities for disabled people: those in wheelchairs; those who are blind; those who are deaf.

4 From your fieldwork do you feel that there is a need for the provision of more amenities such as:
   (a) car parks, cafés and public conveniences;
   (b) benches, picnic tables and litter bins;
   (c) maps and signposts?
   Where would you locate the extra amenities? Explain why.

5 Imagine that you have overall responsibility for providing and maintaining leisure facilities in the area you have investigated. Suggest, with reasons such as site, safety or cost, whether you would close some, expand others and introduce new ones.

6 Test one or more of these hypotheses:
   (a) 'That more young people than old people pursue formal activities.'
   (b) 'That young people pursue a greater variety of activities than children or older people do.'
   (c) 'That formal leisure facilities are expensive to provide, and planners should direct their spending to the provision of a greater number/area of informal facilities.'

FURTHER SUGGESTIONS

For suggestions 1 and 2 you will need to return to the leisure area and continue your investigation using methods identical to those used the first time.

1

Choose a day and time constrasting to the first investigation, perhaps a weekend afternoon or a weekday morning, and repeat the investigation. The proportions of people using the leisure facilities may be quite different. Illustrate your results and then describe similarities and contrasts between the two investigations. From your own knowledge, suggest reasons for these.

2

Find out whether the weather affects the use of the facilities. You may have forgotten details of weather conditions during your first investigation so look up details in a newspaper for that day. Copies are kept in public libraries. Plan a repeat study for a day forecast to have different weather conditions. Note both the forecast and the actual weather.

It is interesting to ask a random sample of people in the area for their own description of the weather on the day. What is 'warm' or 'mild' to one person may be 'cold' to another; 'bracing' or 'invigorating' to some may be 'wild' and 'gale-force' to others!

Illustrate the results of your fieldwork as you did for the earlier study, using exactly the same scale. For purposes of comparison between the two studies, set your diagrams alongside each other and describe similarities and differences between them. How have weather conditions affected the results?

Since these two further suggestions will probably involve different numbers of people, the results could be well illustrated as proportional circles (see pages 61–2).

2 : To investigate the impact of public use upon a leisure area

PREPARATION

How is an area of land altered to provide leisure facilities? Consider the facilities that you expect to find in the area you are about to investigate. How has the landscape been altered to provide these? Make a note of alterations such as creating undulating land for a golf course; damming a stream to provide a lake for toy boats; draining marshland and building embankments for a promenade along a sea front; location of swings and other play equipment; location of benches.

What effect do people using leisure facilities have upon the area? From this short list pick out any which you think may apply in the area you have chosen to investigate, and add your own suggestions:

grass is worn away on pitches used for games;
footpaths are eroded near to a bridge or stile, or close to the entrance of a car park;
graffiti on signs;
litter;
signposts, stone walls or fences are damaged;
'souvenirs' such as pebbles, pieces of stalactites, small plants are collected;
signposts are turned to point in the wrong direction.

When your list is as long as possible you will probably realise that every item causes some form of damage. Some of the damage is absolutely unintentional and almost unavoidable. Other damage is intentional and so must be classed as vandalism. Separate your lists into the two different kinds, and be alert to both during your fieldwork.

Some types of damage such as the breaking of windows, chasing of sheep or erosion of footpaths are difficult to assess during fieldwork, so write to ask for information on these from the Parks and Gardens Department of an urban area, the Warden of a Country or National Park or the Chief Keeper at a Zoo.

Sometimes there are signs of neglect, perhaps because of lack of money for repairs. Signs, buildings and fences may need painting, for example.

Copy the Leisure Landscape Assessment Scheme.

LEISURE LANDSCAPE ASSESSMENT SCHEME		
Very pleasant/very attractive	=	5
Pleasant/quite attractive	=	4
Acceptable/reasonable	=	3
Not very pleasant	=	2
Unpleasant/unattractive	=	1

EQUIPMENT
- **Basic fieldkit** including base-map of scale 1:2500 of the fieldwork area
- **Tape measure** or **metre rule**
- **Leisure Landscape Assessment Scheme**

FIELDWORK METHOD
The fieldwork falls into three main sections.

I Assessment of the quality of the leisure landscape
Walk along each road and path on the map, and, pacing yourself at intervals – 10 m, 25 m, 50 m or 100 m appropriate to the changes in the landscape, including difference in facilities – stop, place a * in the appropriate place on the map and observe the attractiveness of the landscape around you. Record your impressions by taking a value from the Leisure Landscape Assessment Scheme.

Remember that none of your fieldwork should ever be destructive.

2 Recording of instructions to the public

Record every sign which gives instructions as to how the public must behave. Write such instructions on the map in the correct location or use an abbreviation, adding this to the map key.

3 Recording of damage or neglect to the facilities

Record the location and type of any damage, including those listed in your preparation. If it is possible to do so without causing inconvenience to anyone, measure the width of an unsurfaced footpath close to a gate or stile, and again about 25 m or more away. Note on your map the width at each location.

PROCESSING THE INFORMATION

1 Map of landscape attractiveness

Trace the 1:2500 scale map of your fieldwork area. Choose a different colour for each landscape assessment such as red for 5, blue for 4 and so on, and make a key. Draw pencil lines to represent the boundaries between areas of different values as accurately as you can and then shade the areas within each boundary in your chosen colour.

2 Distribution map of instructions to the public

Make a list of all the different instructions recorded on your fieldwork map. Some may have been recorded more than once so place a √ beside the instruction each extra time it occurs.

Look at your fieldwork map. Are the instructions grouped in particular areas or fairly evenly spread around? Where there is a grouping place a black line around its location on your map of landscape attractiveness. Include this in the key. Can you suggest why so many instructions are needed here, and fewer elsewhere? Write down your suggestions.

Describe any link you see between your landscape assessment value and the location of groupings of instructions.

3 Tracing overlay of damage to the leisure area

Make two lists of the different types of damage recorded, using these headings:

UNINTENTIONAL DAMAGE
DELIBERATE DAMAGE

If a type occurs more than once, place a √ beside it each extra time.

Decide upon a symbol for each type of damage.

Make a **tracing overlay**, as described on page 50, to cover your Map of Landscape Attractiveness. Locate the sites of damage by symbols on the tracing paper. Add the key.

4 Assessment of the effectiveness of instructions to the public

Look at your map and tracing overlay. Describe any relationship you see between areas of damage and the degree of attractiveness. Do 'damage' symbols on the map occur close to the rings which represent groupings of instructions to the public?

Describe whether you consider that the instructions help to prevent damage. Are there, in your opinion, too many or too few instructions? Can you suggest improvements?

5 Comparisons between leisure areas

If you have investigated two or more small leisure areas add up the values given for each Leisure Landscape Assessment and divide the total of each by its area to find the average assessment value. Compare the averages to see whether they correspond to your overall impression of each. Can you see a link between the amount of damage you have recorded and the average assessment value? Describe how effective you consider the instructions to the public to be in each area.

DRAWING CONCLUSIONS

1 Describe what your investigations show about the use and abuse of leisure facilities.
2 Imagine that you have been brought in as an adviser to improve the attractiveness of the leisure area. What suggestions would you make?
3 A new motorway is to open within the next five years. This is estimated to bring a quarter of a million visitors to a previously unspoiled area of country or coastline. Drawing upon your fieldwork, devise a leisure area of 6 square kilometres designed to minimise damage and thus conserve the attractiveness of the landscape while providing the best of facilities for all age-groups.
4 Test one or more of these hypotheses:
   (a) 'That most damage in a leisure area is deliberate.'
   (b) 'That the alteration of certain facilities would improve the quality of the landscape and lower the possibilities of damage.'
   (c) 'That the landscape would be better conserved if the leisure area were extended.'

FURTHER SUGGESTION

Choose a small urban park and investigate it in the same way as you did the larger area. Compare your results.

3 : To investigate where visitors come from and the effects of visitor traffic upon the road network

PREPARATION

How do people reach a leisure area? Some come by public transport, but most travel in private motor cars or coaches. Each car in this country is estimated to carry an average of 3.2 passengers. Find out how many passengers different types of coaches and minibuses carry.

Find out how well your chosen leisure area is served by public transport. Write to the person in charge of the leisure area or to the local Tourist Information Office and ask for timetables.

Private motorists may be concerned about the cost of petrol and this could limit the distance they would travel to a leisure area and the roads they would use. Others consider journey-time of greater importance than petrol costs, and improvements in access by road are welcomed. An example of this is that when the M62 motorway was completed 12½ million people were within 1½ hours' drive (at 90 kph) and 16 million within 2 hours' drive of the Yorkshire Dales National Park.

Trace a map of the roads leading from the nearest towns to the area you intend to investigate. Choose a scale of map appropriate to your estimation of the size of the catchment area of visitor's homes: 1:25 000 or bigger for a park in a built-up area; 1:250 000 for one or more entrances to a National Park.

Draw a topological map of the roads which serve the leisure area. This will help you to assess, before your fieldwork, how efficient they are likely to be as routes of access to the leisure area.

Represent the leisure area and the surrounding settlements as nodes/vertices and the roads as arcs/edges.

Figure 7 Conventional and topological maps to show access to a leisure area

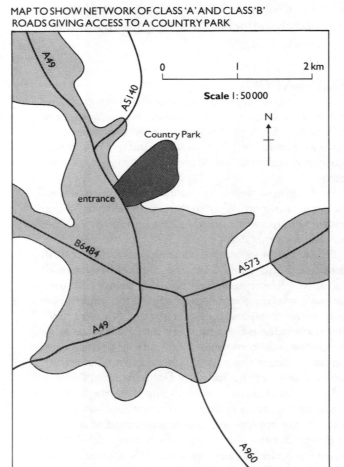

MAP TO SHOW NETWORK OF CLASS 'A' AND CLASS 'B' ROADS GIVING ACCESS TO A COUNTRY PARK

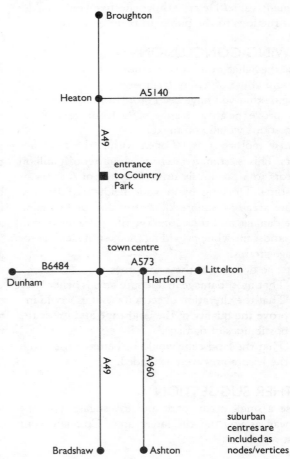

TOPOLOGICAL MAP OF THE SAME AREA

Key

built-up areas

On the example in figure 7 these are shown as dots and straight lines, respectively. Decide where you will make traffic counts to investigate the roads most heavily used.

Visitors' books and hotel registers often give information about where people came from. Before beginning your fieldwork write to the person in charge – the proprietor or manager – asking if you may see the hotel register on the date of your fieldwork, but at a time convenient to him/her. Explain which school you are from, and the reason why you wish to see the register. These registers will probably reveal peak visiting times which may be a Bank Holiday Weekend or a special sailing contest. Take this into consideration when choosing the date for your fieldwork. Busy days produce better results. Also bear in mind that the peak visiting time of day is often between 1530 h and 1700 h.

Copy the Journey to Leisure Area Questionnaire (page 16) and the Table for Recording Traffic Count (page 17). The table has been partly filled in to show you how to do it.

EQUIPMENT
- **Basic fieldkit** including a base-map of scale 1:50 000
- **Questionnaire** – Journey to Leisure Area
- **Table for Recording Traffic Count** (4 copies)

FIELDWORK METHOD

1 Observation of the access route
On your journey to the fieldwork location make a note, preferably at the appropriate place on the map, of the ways in which roads are affected by traffic. Consider the road surface itself, traffic jams in towns and inconvenience to people living in the area caused by increased traffic and petrol fumes.

The Police Force, AA, RAC and the Tourist Information Centre will supply details of the effects of such things as repairs and traffic jams on roads. Write to one of them requesting information.

2 Survey of parked cars
Make a survey of parked cars to see where they have come from. The most reliable way of telling where a vehicle has come from is to record the place named on the road tax disc displayed on the windscreen. Most people pay road tax at a Post Office close to their home, or directly to Swansea where the Driving Vehicle Licensing Centre issues a computer-printed disc. Provided that only a small percentage of vehicles have these discs, your survey will still be accurate.

If an attendant is on duty ask his/her permission to record the place named on the road tax discs, or if the car park belongs to a café ask permission of the proprietor or manager. Also assure the person that you will not touch any vehicle.

Note the date and the time of survey, and the six-figure grid reference of the car park, then systematically record in your field notebook the places on the car tax discs. If a place occurs more than once put a √ beside it each extra time.

If there is a separate coach park carry out an identical survey there.

If there is a vast number of cars it may be sensible to take a **systematic random sample** by recording every third, fifth or even tenth car. Decide upon the interval and keep to it accurately. Note the reason for taking only a sample and how you carried it out.

3 Questionnaire
Carry out a survey of where people have come from, using the questionnaire. Unless it is an extremely quiet day you will have to take a **systematic random sample** from people. Ensure that you really do interview every

JOURNEY TO LEISURE AREA QUESTIONNAIRE

NAME OF SCHOOL:.................................

DATE:....................   TIME:..................

As part of the geography course the use of this leisure area (Name..............)
is being studied. It would help the study if you would please answer the following
questions:

1 What is the name of the town, village or district in which you live?

....

2 Where did you begin your journey today?.................

3 (a) How did you reach the area today?..................
   (b) Please name or give the M.O.T. class and number of the roads you used.

....

4 Did you encounter any problems on the journey?
   If 'YES' please give brief details.....................

....

5 How far do you think you have travelled to reach the area?

....

6 How long did you spend in travelling? (deduct time for deliberate stops on the
way)

....

REMEMBER TO THANK THE PERSON YOU HAVE INTERVIEWED

fifth or tenth or fifteenth person – whichever interval you choose. A mechanical counter would be helpful.

4 Traffic survey on access routes
From your topological map or traced map choose locations at which to investigate the amount of traffic which uses roads leading to the entrance to the leisure area.

If you feel that improvements should be made to the road network it will be important to conduct traffic counts also on the lesser-used roads. Choose your survey location carefully, bearing in mind the effect of a side road or a one-way system already in force.

In a built-up area it may be worthwhile to investigate visitors arriving on foot as well as by some form of transport.

The traffic survey must be conducted in pairs, with one person standing on each side of the road. Synchronise your watches and decide upon the precise time to start the count. If more than one pair is taking part the other pairs should count at exactly the same time on other roads. Record your results in the Table for Recording Traffic Count.

PROCESSING THE INFORMATION

1 Desire-line map(s) of the catchment area of visitors' homes

Use your records from tax discs and questionnaires to draw desire-lines showing where visitors come from. The method for drawing a desire-line map is explained on pages 49–51. Choose a scale appropriate to the distances of the leisure area from visitors' homes.

The answers to question 5 of the Journey to Leisure Area questionnaire could be illustrated on a 'Perceived Distance Desire-Line Map'. Place this for comparison beside a map of 'Actual Distances' for the same people interviewed.

On both maps draw a dashed line around the outside ends of the arrows to show the catchment area of visitors' homes (see figure 10 on page 51). You may calculate the area by following the method explained on page 96.

Describe what your maps show and, if you have also drawn a 'Perceived Distance Map', describe any differences between this and the 'Actual Distance Map'.

TABLE FOR RECORDING TRAFFIC COUNT

IMPORTANT: Counting must last for exactly 10 minutes. At the counting point record only the vehicles which travel on your side of the road.

LOCATION OF COUNT: A 49 between Heaton and entrance to Country Park

DATE:
TIME: 15·45 h

VEHICLES TRAVELLING TOWARDS: Country Park

CAR	COACH	MINIBUS	LORRY	VAN	MOTOR CYCLE	BUS	OTHERS
‖‖‖	‖	‖‖‖	‖‖‖	‖‖‖	‖‖‖	‖	‖‖‖
‖‖‖			‖	‖‖‖			
‖‖‖				‖‖‖			
‖‖‖							
‖							

2 Maps of road density surrounding the leisure area

From an Ordnance Survey map or the tracing you made before you undertook your fieldwork, measure the length of each type of road within your chosen area. Use the 'pin and string' method of measurement explained on page 49. Calculate the area by the method explained on page 96. Express the density as kilometres of road per 100 square kilometres.

Which type of road has the highest density? Rank the others in order of density. Describe which type of road would be capable of taking extra traffic if need be. You may refer to specific roads along which you have travelled and recorded road surface, traffic jams and road works.

3 Flow-line maps to illustrate traffic usage

Draw a large topological map of the road network, and, using the results of your traffic counts and details supplied by an organisation to which you have written draw a flow-line map as explained on page 43. You may distinguish between 'visitor-type' traffic – mainly cars, coaches and minibuses – and 'ordinary' traffic, which includes lorries. Choose the scale with care and add this to your map.

4 Isochrone map of journey time from home to leisure area

On a tracing of the Ordnance Survey map use the record of answers to questions 1 and 6 of the questionnaire to plot the location of the visitors' homes and the length of time taken to reach the leisure area. If more than one person came from a particular place but with a different journey-time, calculate the average journey-time. As in the imaginary example below, join lines of equal journey-

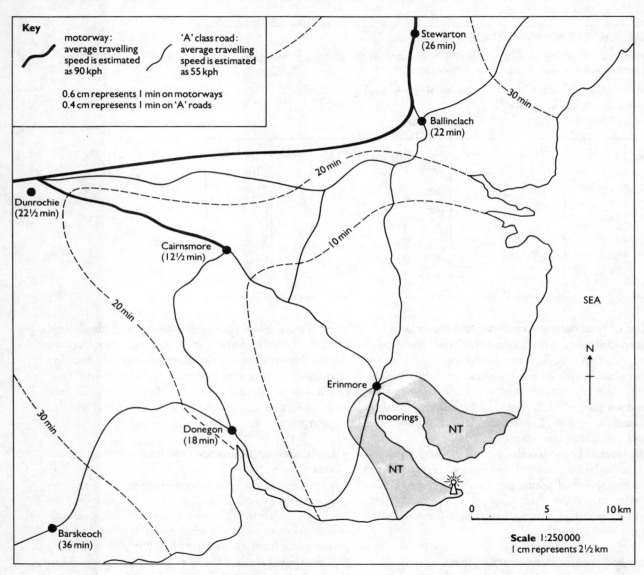

Key

motorway: average travelling speed is estimated as 90 kph

'A' class road: average travelling speed is estimated as 55 kph

0.6 cm represents 1 min on motorways
0.4 cm represents 1 min on 'A' roads

Stewarton (26 min)

30 min

Ballinclach (22 min)

20 min

Dunrochie (22½ min)

10 min

Cairnsmore (12½ min)

20 min

SEA

N

Erinmore

moorings

NT

Donegon (18 min)

30 min

NT

Barskeoch (36 min)

0   5   10 km

Scale 1:250 000
1 cm represents 2½ km

Figure 8 Isochrone map to show journey time by motorways and 'A' class roads to Erinmore National Trust Area

time. These lines are called **isochrones**.

For planning purposes you should draw a theoretical isochrone map of the area, measuring distances along the quickest routes in the network. Assume that passenger vehicles average the following speeds:

90 kph on motorways

55 kph on 'A' class roads

40 kph on 'B' class and minor roads.

Write a description to compare the 'observed' isochrone map and the theoretical isochrone map. If there are some major contrasts between the two maps, suggest reasons for these. The next map may help you to add more detailed reasons.

5 Topological map to show problems for motorists

Draw your topological map again. Devise a key suited to the kinds of disruptions that have occurred on the roads during your fieldwork. Use your own observations, those given by interviewees in answer to question 4 of the questionnaire, and details supplied by the organisation to which you have written.

DRAWING CONCLUSIONS

1 From your investigations, describe the catchment area of the homes of visitors to the leisure area. Suggest reasons for this in terms of the transport used, journey-time and cost.

2 Imagine that you are a member of the local council and have been asked to review the road network serving the leisure area. First describe the existing conditions, including all problems to (a) people visiting the leisure area, (b) local inhabitants, (c) through-traffic. Next suggest, with illustrations, different ways in which improvements could be made.

3 Test one or more of these hypotheses:

(a) 'That congestion in the road network surrounding the leisure area could be relieved by the pro-

vision of a smaller leisure area approximately midway between the edge of the existing catchment area and the leisure area investigated.'

(b) 'That the provision of park-and-ride facilities (free car park plus frequent minibus service) at a distance from the areas of outstanding interest would (a) enhance the interest and (b) reduce the cost of road maintenance within the leisure area.'

(c) 'That public transport facilities to the leisure area should be increased.'

FURTHER SUGGESTIONS

1

Carry out investigations at an Indoor Leisure Centre and compare your findings with those of the Outdoor Leisure Area you have studied.

2

Investigate the cost of the journey to the leisure area in relation to the popularity of the facilities provided.

VILLAGE/SMALL TOWN

A settlement is any building made by people upon the land. Villages and towns are clusters of buildings, usually with some open spaces such as parks, tennis courts or bowling greens. In this chapter the settlement will always be called a village.

Every settlement has a **shape**, which is sometimes called its **form** or **lay-out**. This is the pattern made by the buildings, streets and open spaces. Within a village there may be areas distinctive because of their function, which in turn influence their·pattern of buildings. The form is also affected by the relief and drainage of the area. The study of form is called **morphology**.

The form of a village may be affected by its development through time. History may be seen in details of buildings: the materials used for building and architectural style. The function of some buildings may have changed several times.

The main function of a village is residential, and some villages have a strong community spirit. One village may be growing in size while another is decreasing. If you investigate several villages in the same area you may be able to arrange them into an order of importance called a **hierarchy**. You may know about one of these theories: Central Place Theory; The Rank-Size Rule of Settlements.

FIELDWORK AREA

As an approximate guide, two people may make an interesting investigation of a village of up to 2000 inhabitants or 750 buildings. A very small village may not show results as clearly.

I : To observe in detail the form and functions of the village

PREPARATION

Geographers find it difficult to decide whether a settlement is a village or a small town. This is made more difficult by the fact that people in large towns often still refer to their local shopping centre as 'the village'. To help you to decide whether the settlement you intend to investigate is a village or a town make two lists headed 'Village' and 'Town' and write down the number and types of functions such as shops, schools, factories which you would *expect* to find in each settlement type. Some functions may occur in both.

Copy the list of shop types from pages 35–6 and the list of types of land in a village below.

TYPES OF LAND USE IN A VILLAGE

B   = Bank
B_1 = Building Society
C   = Caravan site; if in use count and record the number of caravans and estimate how many more could be parked there
D   = Public house (not residential)

E_1 = Cinema

E_2 = Village hall, including Scout and Guide huts, Women's Institute

E_3 = Bingo hall, if separate building

F = Farmed land, including paddock for riding horses

F_s = Riding school and riding stables

G = Cemetery

H = Doctor's surgery, health centre or clinic, dentist

H_1 = Hospital

I = Optician

L_1 = Bowling green including clubhouse

L_2 = Cricket ground including clubhouse

L_3 = Football ground including clubhouse

L_4 = Public garden, including children's recreation ground

L_5 = Tennis courts

O_g = Local Government Offices

O = Other offices: those which provide a professional service such as a solicitor or accountant

P = Police station

R = Inhabited house

R_a = House used for only part of the year as a holiday home

RH = Residential hotel, including Bed and Breakfast accommodation

SP = Primary school

SS = Secondary school

T = Public car park

T_1 = Bus stop

T_2 = Bus station

T_3 = Railway station. Record TX if the station is unused

U = Unused or derelict land

W = Place of worship. Note the type: C. of E., R.C., Meth., U.R.C., and any other denominations

X = Library

Z = Mill or factory. ZX if unused

EQUIPMENT

- **Basic fieldkit** including map of scale 1:1250 or 1:2500
- **List of Shop Types**
- **List of Types of Land Use in a Village**

FIELDWORK METHOD

With your sketch-map walk along both sides of every street and lane which has buildings along it, and record the use at the ground-level storey of buildings and that of open land. Refer to the list of 'Types of Land use in a Village' and to the 'List of Shop Types', and write over every building and open space on your map the most appropriate letter and/or number. Mark in any new buildings or new divisions of land not shown on your map, and cross out buildings which have been demolished.

PROCESSING THE INFORMATION

1 Sketch-map to show the importance of different types of land use (functions) in the village

Classify into categories the different types of land use recorded. Some functions could be placed in more than one category, so decide, with reasons, which is the most appropriate. Shade the land use in different colours on your map as suggested in the table on page 22.

2 Calculating the importance of different types of land use in the village

Arrange the functions in their rank order. Calculate each as a percentage of the total recorded in order to easily and accurately compare this village with others of different size.

3 Bar-chart to show the importance of different types of land use in the village

Draw a bar-chart of the percentage of different types of

FUNCTION	NUMBER RECORDED	COLOUR ON MAP	RANK ORDER	% OF TOTAL
RESIDENTIAL	649	YELLOW	1	85
SHOPS	53	GREEN	2	7
COMMUNITY ACTIVITIES	21	RED	3	3
PROFESSIONAL SERVICES	12	BLUE	4	1·6
ENTERTAINMENT	11	ORANGE	5	1·4
OPEN SPACES	10	GREY	6	1·3
WORK	5	BROWN	7	0·7
TOTAL BUILDINGS AND DIVISIONS OF LAND RECORDED	761			

land use, starting with the largest percentage at the left. Shade each bar in the same colour as used on the map. Add a key to the colours used.

Describe what the table and the bar-chart show about the importance of the different functions in the village as a whole.

4 Distinguishing functional areas on the sketch-map by using a tracing overlay

Draw a dashed line around the built-up area on your map. Having already coloured the map, you may be able to pick out groupings of particular functions within the dashed line and to give each a descriptive name such as 'the shopping area'.

To help you to see functional areas in a big village make a tracing overlay of your coloured map as described on page 25. On the tracing paper draw a grid by dividing each 100 m grid square on the map into four small squares, the sides of which represent 50 m.

Decide upon the main land use type (function) in each small square and colour the tracing paper square in the same colour. Leave the roads unshaded.

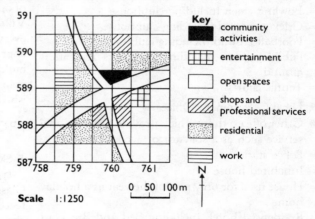

Figure 1 *50-metre grid line map to show functional areas in a village*

Write a sentence to describe the shape made by the dashed-line surrounding the village.

Describe the **functional areas** you can pick out either from the map or from the tracing overlay. To locate each functional area by its place within the village divide the map into four:

$$\frac{NW \mid NE}{SW \mid SE},$$

or give the six-figure grid reference of the middle of each functional area.

DRAWING CONCLUSIONS

1 Describe what your observations and calculations based on the maps and diagrams show about the form and functions of the village.
2 Describe any outstandingly important function in the village and suggest possible reasons for it.
3 If you would like to live in this village choose the house you would prefer and explain the reasons why.
4 Imagine that in a competition you have won a two-week visit to the village. Describe how you would spend your time, say which amenities you would use and suggest which others you feel should be there.
5 Use your observations and calculations to test one or more of these hypotheses:
   (a) 'That a large village has more amenities for its inhabitants than a small village.'
   (b) 'That a village must have more than 150 buildings before it is possible to recognise different functional areas.'
   (c) 'That there are too few shops and amenities for the number of homes in the village.'
   (d) 'That the establishment of a hypermarket on the outskirts would have widespread effects upon the village and its inhabitants.'

FURTHER SUGGESTION

Is the village sited on flat land, on a hill-top or on sloping land? To remind yourself, look again at your fieldwork map and mark an arrow pointing uphill on the streets sloping upwards. A double arrow can mark a street which is very steep. If you had been a builder at the time the village was begun and, therefore, without modern tools and equipment, would the shape of the land have influenced your decision where to build?
Gradients: A quick method of estimating the gradient by looking at a map of scale 1:25 000 or 1:50 000 is:
(a) where the contours are 1 mm apart the gradient is

1 in 5 = 20%;
(b) where the contours are 2 mm apart the gradient is 1 in 10 = 10%;
(c) where the contours are 0.5 cm apart the gradient is 1 in 25 = 4%.

Section/profile: A section drawn accurately will show relationships between the site and functional areas (page 22). Rule a line on your sketch-map to show exactly where your section is, and then, since contours are not marked on large-scale maps, use one of smaller scale to draw the section. Locate each end of the section with its six-figure grid reference. The method for drawing a section is explained on pages 112–13. Remember to give the vertical exaggeration.

As on the section in figure 2, accurately mark the location of structural areas in your village. Shade these according to the colour code used for your sketch-map.
Geological maps: The solid geology map will show the different rock types, and the drift geology map deposits of sediment, such as boulder clay (till) and alluvium,

Figure 2 Section to show the relationship between site and functional areas in a village

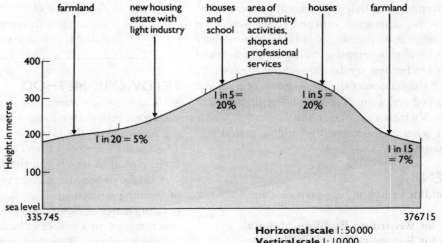

that help to make the site of the village the shape shown in your section. Draw a geological map of the area of the village. Add a key and write a description of what your map shows.

2 : To investigate the development of the village through time

PREPARATION

The Domesday Survey made in AD 1086 shows that 90 per cent of present-day cities, towns and villages of England were already established settlements then. They are recorded in the Domesday Book. Northern Ireland, Scotland and Wales do not have such a complete record from this early date, but it is probable that most settlements everywhere in Britain began more than 1000 years ago.

Before beginning your fieldwork make sure that you know the architectural styles of different periods in history. Before the nineteenth century, roads were poor and travel difficult so that styles of building were very localised. With improvements in transport architectural styles tended to become similar throughout the country according to the fashion of the times. Some of the most easily identified styles are post-World-War II, Inter-war (1918-1940), Victorian and Georgian.

Copy the schemes for recording building period and building materials.

EQUIPMENT

- **Basic fieldkit** including base-map of scale 1:1250 or 1:2500
- **Scheme for Recording Building Materials**
- **Scheme for Recording Building Period**

SCHEME FOR RECORDING BUILDING PERIOD

NEW = Since World War II

INT = Inter-war Period (1918–1940)

VIC = Victorian

GEO = Georgian

OLD = older than Georgian

SCHEME FOR RECORDING BUILDING MATERIALS

 A building mainly of brick

 A building mainly of stone

 A building mainly of timber

 A building of materials of which you are uncertain: cement-covered, pebble-dashed, colour-washed or painted

---

FIELDWORK METHOD

Walk along every street and lane with buildings on it shown on your sketch-map. As you come to each building record, as in the lists,

1 the main materials of which it is built, and
2 the period in which you think it was built.

A bridge or viaduct may have a stone with the date of building written upon it. Record this and also the building material. Sometimes the date is also marked on one house or on a terrace of houses, and names such as 'Jubilee Row' and 'Waterloo Terrace' can give a clue to the period in which they were built. Be sure to find out which jubilee is recorded and the date of the battle!

You may be able to buy a local history guide from the parish church, or write to the secretary of the nearest local history society asking for a guide. Old maps and photographs will give extra evidence of the village's development, and you may be able to copy them. The priest, vicar or minister of the parish church and the person in charge of the Post Office may know a lot about changes in the village, particularly in recent years. They are busy people so write beforehand, tell them which school you are from and why you would like to interview them.

PROCESSING THE INFORMATION

1 Sketch-map and description of historical development

Make a neat copy of your sketch-map and shade each building in colour in the method suggested on page 22. Use the most striking colours for the oldest buildings and use a different colour for each building period. Add this as the key.

It may be helpful to have only the oldest buildings shaded on the map, and use tracing overlays for each period in succession so that you 'build up' the village as in figure 3.

Describe what your maps show, and add any extra information that you have, referring to its source: 'the Parish Church Guide-Book' or 'photographs in the village library'.

2 Sketch-map of building materials

Either on your neat map of historical development, or on a separate map, shade each building according to its main building materials. Line shading in black ink will enable you to see the colour of the building period below if you do it on the same map. Different materials can be shown like this:

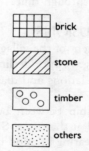

or use the key on page 24. Add the key to your map.

3 Correlation between building period and building materials

Count the total number of buildings of each building period, and then, within each period (Old, Georgian

Figure 3 Tracing overlays to show the development of the village through history

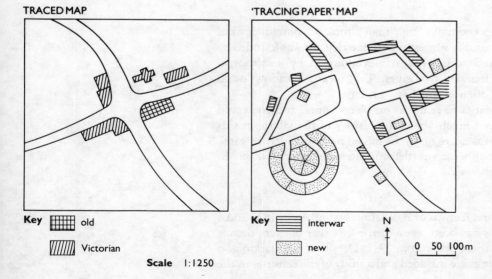

TRACED MAP

Key ▦ old
▨ Victorian

Scale 1:1250

'TRACING PAPER' MAP

Key ▤ interwar
⬚ new

N

0 50 100m

etc.), count the total number of buildings made mainly of stone and then of brick and lastly of timber. Make a note of each number. Draw a cumulative bar-chart as on page 103 to represent the total number of buildings of each period, starting with the oldest at one side and working across to the most recent. Shade each in the colour used on your map and tracing overlays. Next line-shade in black ink over each bar, the number of buildings made from that material.

Look for patterns in the building materials used in different periods. If you calculate the number of each building material type as a percentage of the total number of buildings of each period it will give a more reliable pattern.

4 Description of changes in building materials used in the village through history

Write a description of the links you see between building materials used in different building periods. Use your sketch-maps and bar-chart as illustration. Try to suggest reasons for any changes through time.

DRAWING CONCLUSIONS

1 Describe the development of the village through history, noting the rapid growth or decline at any time, using your maps, calculations and diagrams as illustration.
2 Describe the relationship between building period and the materials used at that time. Suggest reasons for any correlations, bearing in mind the availability of building materials, transport and the technical knowledge of the times.
3 Imagine that you will return to the village in 100 years' time. Which parts of the village would you like to see remaining, and which would you demolish or improve? How would you try to ensure the preservation of your chosen parts of the village?

4 Imagine that you are in charge of entering the village in a competition for the 'Best-kept village'. Plan the judges' tour of inspection so that areas of historical interest as well as new areas of development are seen to best advantage. What suggestions would you give to make the village as attractive as possible?
5 Test one or more of these hypotheses:
(a) 'That before 1940 most buildings in the village were constructed from local materials.'
(b) 'That the oldest buildings are located close to the village centre, and buildings become progressively more recent outwards.'
(c) 'That buildings of historical interest should be preserved for future generations.'
(d) 'That the village is attractive to the eye as well as practically convenient as a place of residence and services.'

FURTHER SUGGESTIONS

1

Names ending in 'ing', 'ham', 'ton', or combinations of these usually suggest that the settlement was founded by Anglo-Saxons, whilst names ending in 'by' and 'thorpe' were founded by Danes. 'Ley' means 'meadows', and 'gate' often meant 'way' or 'lane'.

Libraries have books on place names, and you could find out much about the history of the village in this way. Take care not to be misled by words such as 'gate', which in a large settlement often *does* refer to a gate in the city wall.

2

The first Census of Population was taken in 1801 and a census has been taken in the first year of every decade since then, apart from 1941. Details of population and buildings are included and a study of the censuses in the nearest public library will show trends in the village since 1801. Note that the figures given include the whole parish and not the village alone.

3

Discover where building stones were quarried and where different bricks and roofing materials were obtained. Show the source of building materials on a map, probably of a smaller scale than that used in your fieldwork. Discover how the materials were transported and the routes used.

From a stone-mason, builder or roofer find out the techniques required for using these materials and describe them.

4

Imagine you are a member of the local Civic Trust. Discover any listed buildings in the village. Make a tracing of the buildings, bridges, walls and gateways that you think should be conserved, and explain why. Do you think that new buildings should be constructed to blend in with the older ones?

5

How would you plan for a new industrial development on the outskirts of the village? Do you think the industrial units should be built so as to blend in with the village? Design any new houses to be built for the people who will work there.

3 : To assess the importance of the village to its surrounding area

PREPARATION

In what ways do you think the village is important to the people who live in the area around it? Make brief notes about the ways in which you feel that the village you are going to investigate may be important to people in farms and other settlements close by.

Parish boundaries are not shown on Ordnance Survey maps of a scale larger than 1:25 000, so copy the parish boundary onto a large-scale map in which the village you intend to investigate is located.

Write to the local clergyman or school headteacher, for example, asking where people come from to use the services of the village. This will help you discover the **catchment area** from which people come to use the facilities of the village.

Make copies of the List of Types of Land Use in a Village (pages 20–1), the List of Shop Types (pages 35–6), the recording sheet for Vehicle Place of Origin (page 29), Questionnaire of Village Importance (page 28) and the recording sheet for the Public Transport Passenger Count (page 29).

EQUIPMENT

- **Basic fieldkit** including base-map of scale 1:1250 or 1:2500 with the parish boundary drawn in
- **List of Types of Land Use in a Village**
- **List of Shop Types**
- **Table for Vehicle Place of Origin**
- **Questionnaire of Village Importance**
- **Table for Passenger Counts**

FIELDWORK METHOD

The fieldwork is best done in stages.

1 Plotting observations on the map

With your map walk along every street and as you come to each building and open space record its function according to Types of Land Use in a Village and to the List of Shop Types.

QUESTIONNAIRE OF VILLAGE IMPORTANCE

Pupils from _____ school are carrying out a survey to assess the importance of _____ (village/town). Would you please help our investigation by answering the following questions? Please answer the first three questions as 'Very good', 'Good', 'Adequate', 'Poor', Very poor'. Write the
    5   4   3   2   1
appropriate value-number in the space beside the question.

(a) What is your opinion of the shops and professional services, e.g. doctor?

(b) What is your opinion of the entertainment facilities, e.g. clubs, societies?

(c) Is the village easily accessible from the surrounding area, e.g. public transport; number of car parks?

(d) Do you prefer this village to others close by (name some)?
    Put a ring around the answer.   'Yes' or 'No'
    In which order would you place the following reasons for preferring this (or another) village?
                                                    Order of preference:
    1. Familiarity
    2. Types of housing available
    3. General appearance of the village
    4. Public transport
    5. Other factors e.g. availability of gas

    Are there any other reasons why you like the village?

(e) Were you born within 5 km (3 miles) of this village?
    Put a ring around the answer.   'Yes' or 'No'

REMEMBER TO THANK THE PERSON YOU HAVE INTERVIEWED

2 Interviewing

Many people will be helpful:

(a) The headteacher of each *school* in the village will be able to tell you the furthest places from which pupils come to school and the clergyman of each *church* will know the places from which the members of the congregation come. You may ask to see Anglican churches' Electoral Rolls, Non-conformist churches' Lists of Members and Roman Catholic churches' Parish Censuses. The catchment area may vary for different schools and different church denominations. Extra evidence may be obtained by discovering where people come from for social activities connected with the school and church.

(b) The secretaries of local *clubs and societies* may tell you where their members come from and in a *residential hotel* the manager may allow you to look at the register. Ask which are the most popular weeks for visitors and discover the places from which all of the visitors came in one of those weeks.

(c) An *estate agent* may be able to give you information about where commuters who buy houses from him go to work, and the most popular method of transport used by them.

(d) At a *livestock market* ask in the office if you may have a catalogue of a recent special sale such as the Lamb Sale. The farms which sold animals will be listed.

(e) Call at the local *garage*, ask if motor repairs are done and from what area the customers come.

(f) If there are many people on the streets, stand where many pass by and take a **systematic random sample**: every third, fifth or tenth person. Politely ask them to answer the questionnaire.

3 Investigation of transport

Investigate the volume of public transport from the village by finding out how frequent the bus and train services are, and whether the frequency varies at different times of the day. Find out the destination of the buses and trains, and, if possible, where each has come from.

Choose a busy time of day, such as early morning or early evening for commuters, mid-morning for shoppers. Using the Public Transport Passenger Count table, stand close to a main bus stop or to the railway station and count and record the number of people getting off each vehicle. If you are working in a pair, also record the number boarding. Note where the transport has come from and where it is going to.

To discover how many people have come by private vehicle, go to each car park, locate it on your map and count and record the number of vehicle spaces. Discover where each vehicle has come from as described on page 15 and record it on the Vehicle Place of Origin table.

If the village is a tourist centre there may be a separate parking area for coaches. Count the number of coach-spaces and look at the rear of the coach for its place of origin. Record all vehicles on your table.

PROCESSING THE INFORMATION

1 **Calculating the percentage of the parish population living in the village**

Look up the population of the village in the AA Members' Handbook, and discover the population of the whole of the parish including that of the village in the Census of Population. Calculate the percentage of people in the parish who live in the village.

PUBLIC TRANSPORT
PASSENGER COUNT BY PUPILS FROM _____ SCHOOL

LOCATION OF COUNT: _____ TIME: _____

PASSENGERS ALIGHTING TRANSPORT FROM _____	PASSENGERS BOARDING TRANSPORT TO _____	TOTAL PASSENGERS COUNTED:
TOTAL:	TOTAL:	

VEHICLE PLACE OF ORIGIN				
PLACE OF ORIGIN	NUMBER OF CARS	NUMBER OF COACHES	OTHER VEHICLES	SWANSEA
Whitethorn	HHT HHT II		III (livestock removal vans from Chippington)	I
Chippington	HHT II			
Birmingham	III	I	II (lorries from Townsend)	
Nottingham	IIII	I	I (caravan from Manchester) TOTAL = 6	

2 Desire-line map to discover the sphere of influence of the village

Trace the boundary of the Civil Parish from a small-scale map, such as the 1:50 000, or even the 1:250 000. Mark the centre of the village as a dot and add desire-lines from the furthest distance travelled from all directions for people using the school, church, clubs and societies, shops and professional services.

Use a different colour of desire-line for each of the facilities plotted: yellow for school, green for shops and professional services and so on. Add a key to the colours. Your map may look similar to the one on page 50.

Place tracing paper over your desire-line map and mark with a dot the beginning of the longest desire-lines irrespective of the village amenity which they represent. Join the dots by a dashed line and calculate the area within (the **catchment area**). The method for measuring area is explained on page 96.

Measure the area of the civil parish in the same unit of measurement as that used for the catchment area. Calculate the area of the catchment area as a percentage of that of the parish.

Describe similarities between the length of desire-lines representing the distance travelled to use different amenities. Are they similar for church and for societies? What does the desire-line map suggest about the importance of shopping and professional services?

Look at the percentage of the population of the parish which lives in the village. From this figure state whether you would expect the sphere of influence to be large or small. Describe whether the percentage of the area within the parish confirms your expectations.

3 Assessing results of completed questionnaires

Divide the questionnaire into those with 'Yes' in answer to the last question (e), and those with 'No' as the answer. In each group total the values of the answers to (a), (b) and (c) on every questionnaire and calculate the average of them all.

Total the answers given by people to each of the six points in (d), and calculate the average value for each answer.

Illustrate the results of each group of valves as bar-charts and Venn diagrams.

Bar-charts: Draw separate bar-charts for the answers to (d) and place them beside those for (a)-(c). Choose an appropriate title for each set of bar-charts, such as 'Views of people born locally' and 'Views of people from outside'.

Venn diagrams: Draw circles of the same radius and overlap them as in Figure 4. Give each a title and write in the appropriate place the factors important to the people interviewed. The number beside each factor tells you how many people have this opinion.

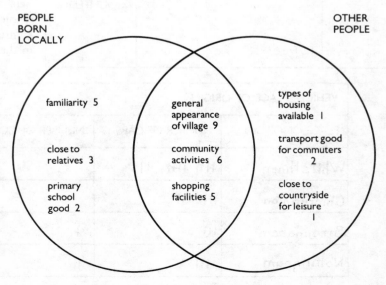

Figure 4 Venn diagram to illustrate the importance of the village to people who live there

PEOPLE BORN LOCALLY

OTHER PEOPLE

familiarity 5

close to relatives 3

primary school good 2

general appearance of village 9

community activities 6

shopping facilities 5

types of housing available 1

transport good for commuters 2

close to countryside for leisure 1

4 Flow-line maps to discover patterns in public transport

If the frequency of public transport services appears to remain constant throughout the day then one diagram will be enough to confirm this. If the frequency varies, divide the day into periods of 3 or 4 hours: 0700 h–1000 h; 1000 h–1400 h; 1400 h–1700 h; 1700 h–1200 h.

Draw separate diagrams to represent bus services and train services. Follow one of the methods described on page 43. Make sure that you show the direction in which the bus or train is moving out from the point at which you counted, and add a key to show the number of buses or trains represented.

5 Tracing overlay to represent passengers

Overlay tracing paper on the flow-line map in the way shown in figure 7 on page 50. Use different colours and different widths to represent the number of passengers alighting and the number boarding (figure 5).

Try to find a key which is appropriate in size to the flow-line map. Give a title to make it clear that the tracing overlay represents people and not vehicles. Add a key to show the number of passengers represented.

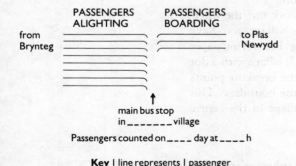

Figure 5 Flow-line map to show public transport passenger movement

6 Graphs of car parks

Using graph paper, take each small square as representing parking space on a car park for one vehicle. Count the total number of squares and rule a line around these. Within this shade the small squares to represent the number of vehicles you counted. If you found a variety of vehicles, such as cars, lorries, coaches, livestock-removal vans, use different colours of shading and add a key.

7 Desire-line map to show place of origin of private vehicles

Trace a small-scale map – 1:50 000 or 1:250 000 – and use the technique shown on page 50 to represent the number of vehicles which have come to the village from a distance and those which are local. To show the variety of vehicles, draw tracing overlays to represent different types of vehicle.

Describe what your desire-line map shows. Does a large proportion of vehicles come from any one direction or place, or are the majority local?

In your opinion are car parking facilities adequate or could they be improved? Do people have to pay for the use of car parks? Do you think this is a good thing or should it be introduced?

DRAWING CONCLUSIONS

1 Using evidence from your fieldwork, consider whether the village has retained its position as the most important place in the parish.
2 Imagine that your family has just bought a house 2 kilometres outside the village. Describe which amenities in the village you would find useful or attractive. Which amenities do you think the village lacks, and where should they be located?
3 Describe, and suggest reasons for the presence of, specialised functions such as livestock market; fish

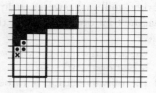

Key

■ car

● livestock removal van

× minibus

Figure 6 Graph paper shaded to show use of a car park

market; mill or brewery; curling rink.

4 Imagine that one or more of the following is to take place:
  (a) the area in which the village is located is to become a National Park;
  (b) the railway station is to be closed;
  (c) people from a nearby city are to be re-housed in new property in the village.
  Consider how the village, the lives of the villagers and of the inhabitants of the surrounding area will be affected.

5 Test one or more of these hypotheses:
  (a) 'That the area of the hinterland/catchment area of the village is greater than that of the civil parish because access by public and private transport is good.'
  (b) 'That the village is mainly a dormitory village because it lacks employment possibilities and is easily accessible to commuters.'

FURTHER SUGGESTIONS

1 Sphere of influence/interaction between neighbouring settlements

The importance of a village is reflected in its sphere of influence, that is, the distance that people will travel to use its shopping and other facilities. The boundary between the spheres of influence of neighbouring settlements is called the 'interaction breaking point'. Some geographers assume that a settlement's facilities should be proportionate to its population. The breaking point between the spheres of influence of neighbouring settlements can be calculated in different ways:

(a) Obtain the population figures for each settlement. On the 1:50 000 map measure the straight-line distance between the settlements, and calculate the breaking point as in figure 7.

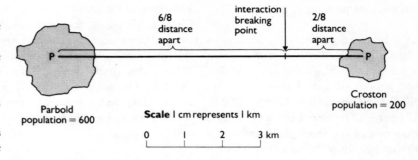

Figure 7 *Diagram to show the interaction breaking point between two villages*

(b) The American geographer W.J. Reilly calculates the breaking point like this:
The breaking point between settlements A and B, when A has the biggest population is

$$\frac{\text{the distance between A and B}}{1 + \sqrt{\left(\dfrac{\text{population of town A}}{\text{population of town B}} \right)}}$$

The distance on the map is measured from the smaller settlement, B.
Do you recognise the resemblance to Newton's Law of Gravity in physics? Reilly's theory has been called 'Reilly's Law of Retail Gravitation'.

Use either method (a) or (b) to work out the interaction breaking point between the village you have investigated and each adjacent village. Put tracing paper over the map. Mark the centre of each village with a dot and draw the breaking point. Join the breaking points together and shade the area inside the boundary. This is the sphere of influence of the village in the centre (figure 8).

2 Central-place theory

If you continue (1) and work out the sphere of influence of each of several settlements in the area you will be able to see how closely your spheres of influence

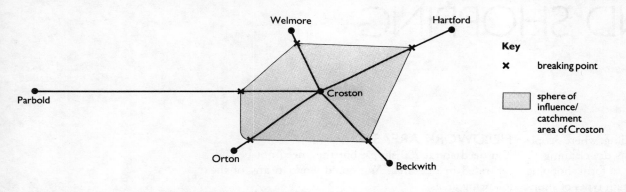

Figure 8 *Map to show the catchment area of Croston by calculating the interaction breaking point*

Key

✗ breaking point

▨ sphere of influence/ catchment area of Croston

approximate to W. Christaller's model. Try to suggest reasons why they may differ in some parts.

3 Comparison of villages with the rank-size theory of settlements

This theory is a hypothesis which states that within an area:

the second biggest settlement has a population ½ the size of the biggest;

the third biggest settlement has a population ⅓ the size of the biggest;

the fourth biggest settlement has a population ¼ the size of the biggest and so on.

Do you see why the name 'rank-size' is given to this hypothesis?

If logarithmic graph paper is used then the perfect rank-size theory of population size is a straight line at 45° between the axes, as in figure 9.

To test the settlements of your area against the hypothetical theory find out the population of each settlement, rank the figures and then plot them on the graph.

Compare the graph of your settlements with the rank-size line: some villages may be bigger and some smaller than in the hypothesis. Suggest reasons for the differences.

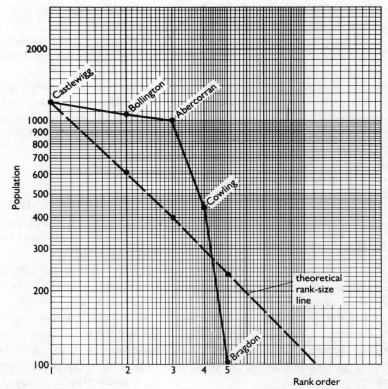

Figure 9 *Rank-size distribution of settlements plotted on logarithmic graph paper*

SHOPS AND SHOPPING

A shop is a building, or part of a building, where people buy goods or pay for a service such as dry-cleaning.

Shops are usually grouped together to form shopping centres. In a big shopping centre, certain types of shops tend to be near each other. In big towns you have probably noticed that department stores and the multiple chain shops are usually on the main streets or in shopping precincts. The rates are often higher there, so there may be a link between the size of the shop and its ability to pay high rates. The appearance of the shop front often reflects the trading standard of the owner and his desire to attract customers.

Have you ever thought how often people go to different shops and where they come from to shop? The area from which people come to the shopping centre is called the **market area**. We tend to buy food frequently and at fairly local shops, whereas expensive goods like furniture are not bought often and we might go further from home to buy them at a shopping centre which has a wider choice of shops. The cost of goods and services and the frequency of shopping enable geographers to place these in an order of importance, called a **hierarchy**. Furniture is thought of as of high status, whereas food is considered of low status. Similarly, the number and variety of shops in different shopping centres may enable us to place them into a hierarchy. Some geographers call shopping centres 'central places', and **central-place theory** is based on their location in relation to one another.

FIELDWORK AREAS

You need about 200 shops, but they need not be concentrated in one area. You could work in any of the following areas:

one shopping street near the centre of a city or large town;
a shopping centre in the suburbs of a large town;
the shopping area in a small town or village;
a shopping precinct;
a hypermarket or very large supermarket.

To make your fieldwork study more interesting you could go to another shopping area. You should then find more patterns and be able to draw more accurate conclusions.

1 : To investigate the number and types of shops in a shopping centre

PREPARATION

Copy the table on page 35 and complete it for your own family and others. The top line has been filled in to show you how to do it.

How many different types of shops are used? Can you see any pattern between the types of goods/shops and their location? Can you explain any patterns in relation to how often the goods are used in the home and how far a family travels to buy them? Is the location of the

GOODS BOUGHT EVERY WEEK	LOCATION OF SHOPS	GOODS BOUGHT EVERY MONTH	LOCATION OF SHOPS	LESS THAN ONCE A MONTH	LOCATION OF SHOPS
fruit	suburban shopping centre	frozen foods	out-of town hypermarket	shoes	town centre

shop related to the cost of the goods? Make a note of your answers to these questions, as you may use them for comparison with the results of your fieldwork.

Copy the following List of Shop Types.

LIST OF SHOP TYPES

The list is numbered in alphabetical order to make plotting in the field easier. No list could be absolutely complete, so add any extra shops you find to the list and give each its own reference number.

The proportion of multiple/chain shops is interesting. Print M beside the reference number. e.g. 7 M, 9 (a) M.

1. Antiques
2. Bookseller and stationer
3. Bread and cakes
4. Café
5. Car showrooms
6. Carpets and furniture
7. Chemist
8. China and glassware
9. Clothes –
   (a) ladies' fashions
   (b) menswear
   (c) children's wear
10. Department store
11. 'Do-it-Yourself' shop, including paints and wallpapers
12. Dress materials, dress patterns, sewing threads
13. Dry cleaner and launderette
14. Electrical showroom
15. Estate agent
16. Fish and game
17. Fish-and-chips, including 'take-away' foods
18. Fishing tackle
19. Flowers and vegetables
20. Food –
    (a) grocer
    (b) small supermarket
21. Gas showroom
22. General store which sells a lot of different goods, usually including some foodstuffs
23. Gardener's shop selling plants, fertilizers and garden tools
24. Gift shop
25. Glass-cutter or glazier
26. Hairdresser
27. Hardware and ironmongery
28. Jewellery
29. Knitting wools, patterns, crochet materials, needles
30. Newspapers, birthday cards, gift wrapping paper
31. Off-licence
32. Post Office
33. Shoes
34. Shoe-repairer
35. Sports equipment

36. Sweets and chocolates
37. Televisions, hi-fi equipment, radios, records, cassettes
38. Tobacco, cigars, lighters, pipes
39. Toys
40. Travel agent

EQUIPMENT

- **Basic fieldkit** including base-map of scale 1:1250
- **List of Shop Types**

FIELDWORK METHOD

Using your base-map, walk along both sides of every street. Look up each shop type as you come to it and write its number on your map, adding M if it is a multiple shop. Mark in any new buildings not shown on your map, and put a cross through any that have been demolished.

PROCESSING THE INFORMATION

1 Sketch-maps

Make a *neat copy* of the sketch-map used in your fieldwork. Name the streets and draw the outline of each building, but omit the reference number.

Classify the shops and professional services into categories and shade each a different colour as suggested:

food shops – red

clothes shops – yellow

household shops selling furniture, hardware, china, glass, televisions, carpets etc. – brown

sports and hobbies shops – green

service shops, including cafés, launderettes, hairdressers, estate agents – orange

Some shops will not fit easily into one category. Call these 'others' or 'miscellaneous' – black

Shade a department store, a hypermarket or a large

HINTS:
A-Z Guides of towns give the names of even the narrowest and smallest streets. Estate agents have detailed maps, and, if you ask politely you may be given one, but make sure that it is drawn to scale.

supermarket in diagonal lines of the colours most appropriate: probably alternate brown and yellow, or red. A shopping precinct which has shops on more than one level will need two or more maps. Label them clearly:

MAP 1 = Upstairs or first-floor level

MAP 2 = Ground-floor or street level

Remember to add a key.

2 Bar-charts and pie-charts

From your fieldwork map count how many shops there are in each category. Each of these can now be made into a percentage of the total number of shops. Percentages are useful if you are going to compare different areas. Next, rank the categories. The category that has the biggest number is ranked Number 1. The next biggest will be ranked 2 and so on. Now draw a bar-chart or pie-chart to show the percentages of the shop categories in your area. Draw your diagram in rank order.

DRAWING CONCLUSIONS

1 Describe what your observations and calculations show about
   (a) the importance of shops as a use of buildings in the area, and
   (b) the importance of different categories of shops.
   Suggest reasons for these conclusions.

2 Use your evidence to test one or more of these hypotheses;
   (a) 'That suburban shopping centres mainly have food shops.'
   (b) 'That main shopping streets in large towns have many chain/multiple shops.'
   (c) 'That hypermarkets sell a very wide variety of goods because there are few shops near to them.'
   (d) 'That there are more clothes shops and household shops than food shops near the centre of a large town.'

(e) 'That family-owned shops tend to be in smaller streets.'

FURTHER SUGGESTION

Repeat your fieldwork in a different type of shopping centre, as suggested in the introduction to this chapter, and describe with reasons, the similarities and differences which you find.

2 : To assess the quality of a shopping centre

PREPARATION

Make as many copies as you think you will need of the Questionnaire for the Assessment of Shopping Centre Facilities.

Using your knowledge of a shopping centre with which you are familiar, complete the questionnaire yourself. Give a numerical value to the answer to each question:

3 = very good;
2 = good;
1 = average;
0 = poor.

EQUIPMENT

- **Basic fieldkit** including base-map of scale 1:1250
- **Questionnaire for the Assessment of Shopping Centre Facilities**

FIELDWORK METHOD

Use the questionnaire and your set of numerical values to discover the views of shoppers. A systematic random sample of every third, fifth or tenth person will overcome any bias on your part towards the interviewees.

QUESTIONNAIRE FOR THE ASSESSMENT OF SHOPPING CENTRE FACILITIES

NAME OF SCHOOL: _____ DATE: _____

As part of the geography course a study of the facilities of this shopping centre is being made. It would help the study if you would please answer 'Very good', 'Good', 'Average' or 'Poor' to each of the following numbered questions.

		Shopper 1	Shopper 2	Shopper 3	Shopper 4	TOTAL
1	The selection of shops					
2	The clustering of shops					
3	Access to public transport					
4	Car parking facilities					
5	The provision of services other than shops, e.g. banks					
6	The separation of pedestrians and traffic, particularly important for the safety of young children and disabled people					
7	Covered walkways and shopping malls					
8	The provision of shrubs, flowers					
	TOTAL					
9	Which part of the shopping area do you regard as the centre?					
10	Can you please suggest any improvements you would like, e.g. more litter bins, department stores, cafés					

REMEMBER TO THANK THE PERSON YOU HAVE INTERVIEWED

PROCESSING THE INFORMATION

1 Bar-charts

Total the values (across) given for each of the first eight questions in turn. Rank the figures and draw a bar-chart with the highest rank first. Describe what it shows about the different qualities of the shopping centre.

For the eight numbered questions total the values (downwards) given by different people interviewed and include your own. Rank these figures, draw a bar-chart and compare the degree to which the views of individual people differ.

2 Mapping the perceived centre of the shopping area

On a map of scale 1:1250 mark the positions of the perceived centres as given by the people you interviewed. Describe your results.

3 Improving the shopping centre

Make a list of all the different suggestions received in answer to question 10. Group the suggestions into categories if possible, and use them as the basis of a report that you could send to a town planner.

DRAWING CONCLUSIONS

1 Which aspect(s) of the shopping centre resulted in the greatest agreement between people and on which aspects was there greatest disagreement?
2 Imagine you are a planner. Describe ways in which you would make the shopping centre more attractive.
3 Test the hypothesis: 'That the quality of the shopping centre could be improved by the provision of further amenities.'

FURTHER SUGGESTION

Make comparisons between the size and quality of other shopping centres.

3 : To investigate the reasons for the location of different types of shop in a shopping centre

PREPARATION

Consider the following questions and then make lists under the headings below. Where are shops of different types located in relation to points of public transport: bus stations and bus stops, railway stations, public car parks? It would be interesting to estimate at the same time how far people are prepared to walk to shops from points of public transport. Which types of shop have their own car parks?

DISTANCE FROM A PUBLIC TRANSPORT POINT		
LESS THAN 50 m	50–100 m	MORE THAN 100 m
groceries	hardware	clothing shops

Can you explain the reasons for this distribution of shops?

Now make lists of the types of shops you think are found in these locations.

ON MAIN STREETS	IN SHOPPING PRECINCTS	ON SIDE STREETS
radio, TV and hi-fi equipment	supermarket	pet shop

Your answers should prove to be guidelines for your fieldwork.

The investigation is best approached from three angles:

1 accessibility for customers;
2 shop rates;
3 customer opinion.

Copy the List of Shop Types on (pages 35–6), the Table for Pedestrian Counts (page 40), part of which has been completed to show you how to do it, the Questionnaire to find out Customer Opinion of Shops and the Table for Recording Shop Type, Length of Street Frontage and Rateable Value (page 41).

EQUIPMENT

- **Basic fieldkit** including base-map of scale 1:1250
- **List of Shop Types**
- **Table for Pedestrian Counts**
- **Table for Recording Shop Type, Length of Street Frontage and Rateable Value**
- **Questionnaire of Customer Opinion of Shops**

FIELDWORK METHOD

1 Measuring accessibility

Accessibility can be measured (a) in distance or (b) in walking time.

(a) Using a different colour or symbol for each transport point, pace distances at 25 and 50 metre intervals along the streets from the transport point and mark these on the map. Go back to your starting point and repeat this in different directions. You may later compare your pacing with the 'map, pin and string method' described on page 49.

(b) Take your map with you and place a coloured dot at the points where you begin to walk from a transport point. Time yourself accurately and at 5 minutes or

QUESTIONNAIRE TO FIND OUT CUSTOMER OPINION OF SHOPS						
Could you please tell me your opinion of this shop in the following four ways:						
SHOP TYPE: television, hi-fi etc.						
Customer	1	2	3	4	5	TOTAL
1. Is it accessible to transport – public transport or car park?	2					
2. Do you think it is near to other shops?	3					
3. Do you find the prices competitive?	3					
4. Do you find the shop attractive?	2					
CUSTOMER TOTAL	10					

HOW TO PACE OUT DISTANCE
Find the length of your average stride to the nearest quarter of a metre by taking average, even strides. Stop on the ball of your 'back' foot with your 'front' foot flat on the ground. A friend can measure with a metre rule or tape measure from the toes of your 'back' foot to the toes of your 'front' foot. Count the number of strides needed to cover 50 metres and/or 100 metres and write this down in your field notebook

other intervals mark a cross.in the same colour as the dot on the map. Remember there will be more people in the streets on certain days and the walking-time will then be longer.

2 Counting pedestrians, customers or cars

A count of pedestrians, customers or cars will provide further information about the accessibility of shops.

Choose a street in each of the three categories shown on your 'distance' map. Stand on the street with a friend and count the people moving in one direction while your friend counts them moving in the opposite direction. Stand close to the buildings: not on the edge

TABLE FOR PEDESTRIAN COUNTS		
LOCATION OF COUNT: outside Betta Shoes	TIME: 1100 h	
PEDESTRIANS MOVING towards the Post Office	PEDESTRIANS MOVING towards the Bus Station	TOTAL IN BOTH DIRECTIONS
₩₩ ₩₩ ₩₩ ₩₩ III	₩₩ ₩₩ II	
TOTAL: 23	TOTAL: 12	35
LOCATION OF COUNT:	TIME:	
PEDESTRIANS MOVING _____	PEDESTRIANS MOVING _____	TOTAL IN BOTH DIRECTIONS
TOTAL:	TOTAL:	

of the pavement. Synchronise your watches, begin the counts exactly together and count for 10 minutes each time. Do not count babies in prams or children obviously below school age.

3 Study of shop rates

A second line of evidence for the location of shops could be their rateable value. Do you think it likely that a shop with a long front on a main street has to pay higher rates than a small shop on a side street? Choose a few shops in different parts of the shopping centre to investigate.

The rates are based on the rateable value of every building decided by the Inland Revenue. The rateable values are available in the local Valuation Department of every Town Hall or County Hall in the country, but it would be sensible first to write a letter to the Officer in Charge of Valuations or to telephone to arrange a time to see them.

To discover whether the rateable value is related to the length of shop front, you will have to measure the shop front either by stepping it out, putting one foot immediately in front of the other, or by pacing it out in strides. Record your findings on the Table for Recording Shop Type, Length of Street Frontage and Rateable Value. Columns 4 and 5 can be completed later.

4 Investigation of customer opinion

For any shop to remain in business it must have a turnover of goods adequate to pay for rates, up-keep of the building and wages for its assistants. The shop must attract customers, and the Questionnaire to Find out Customer Opinion of Shops lists some ways in which they do so. If you can think of more add them.

To find out how successful shops are, choose three shops at different distances from transport points. Mark them on your base-map. Ask several customers for their opinion of the shop's feature according to this point system:

Very good = 3   Average = 1
Good   = 2   Poor   = 0

Record this on the questionnaire. Your results will be more accurate if you take a systematic random sample of customers. Choosing every 5th or 10th customer to leave the shop will avoid the possibility of your choosing only customers whom perhaps you prefer to interview.

PROCESSING THE INFORMATION

1 **Choropleth map of distance/time from points of transport**

On your base-map use the same colour as the dot or

SHOP Number of shop. Name and/or type	SMALL FAMILY OWNED (F) OR CHAIN/ MULTIPLE (M)	LENGTH OF SHOP FRONT			RATEABLE VALUE
		Number of strides/feet	Length of my stride/feet	Total paced/ stepped length	
Sally Lunn (baker and confectioner) No. 23	F	5 strides	× 0.75m	= 2.75m	£600
Betta Shoes 25 - 27	M	8 strides		= 6.0m	£1760
Dunn's Dispensing chemist No. 29	F	4 strides			£725
A. Walker (sports equipment)	F	6½ strides			£1000

TABLE FOR RECORDING SHOP TYPE, LENGTH OF STREET FRONTAGE AND RATEABLE VALUE

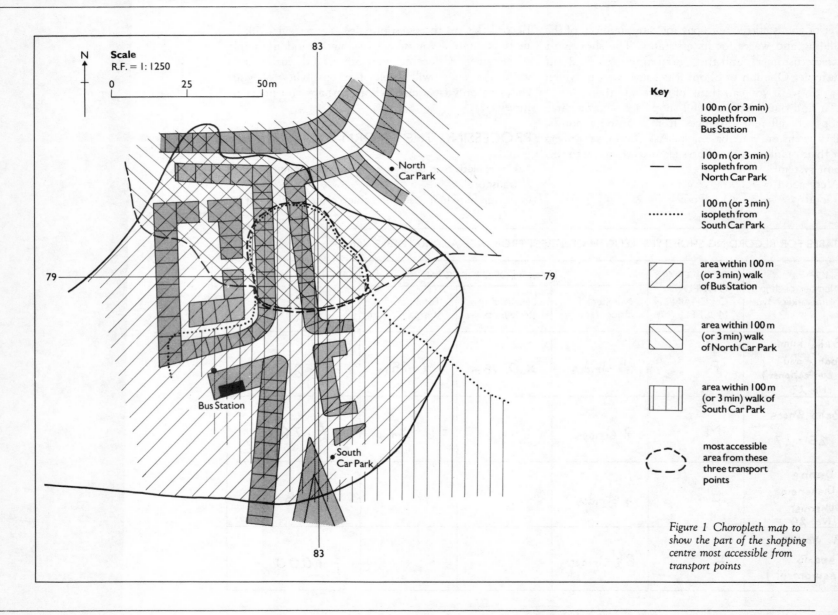

N

Scale
R.F. = 1 : 1250

0   25   50 m

83

● North
Car Park

79   79

Bus Station

South
Car Park

83

Key

100 m (or 3 min)
isopleth from
Bus Station

100 m (or 3 min)
isopleth from
North Car Park

100 m (or 3 min)
isopleth from
South Car Park

area within 100 m
(or 3 min) walk
of Bus Station

area within 100 m
(or 3 min) walk
of North Car Park

area within 100 m
(or 3 min) walk of
South Car Park

most accessible
area from these
three transport
points

*Figure 1 Choropleth map to
show the part of the shopping
centre most accessible from
transport points*

symbol marking your transport point to shade all the buildings within your chosen distance or chosen walking-time from the dot. Now try to draw a line around these buildings. The line is called an **isopleth**. Where the shaded areas overlap is probably the most accessible and, therefore, the most profitable area for shops (figure 1).

2 Flow-line maps

Draw these for the results of your pedestrian, customer and car counts.

What is the largest number of items that you want to represent on your flow-line map? If it is 10 or less you can draw that number of thin lines parallel to one another (figure 2). The arrow-head shows the direction of movement/flow.

If the numbers are bigger, you must make a line represent more people or draw and shade in a thicker line proportionate to the number of people.

3 Accessibility map and rateable value of shops

Locate on the map you drew for accessibility the shops which you investigated for rateable value and shop frontage. Describe any relationship you see between rateable value and accessibility.

4 Diagram and scattergraph: length of shop front and rateable value

Classify the shops into the categories given on page 36 and, placing them in order along the street, draw and colour a diagram as in figure 4 (page 44). Remember to add a key.

Describe any links you see between shop type and length of shop front.

Now, draw a scattergraph and plot your data on it, as in figure 5 (page 46).

Next, draw a best-fit/trend line as follows. Calculate

Key to shops

3	bread and cakes
7	chemist
9c	children's wear
17	fish-and-chips
19	flowers
26	hairdresser
29	knitting wools, etc.
31	off-licence
32	post office
20b	small supermarket

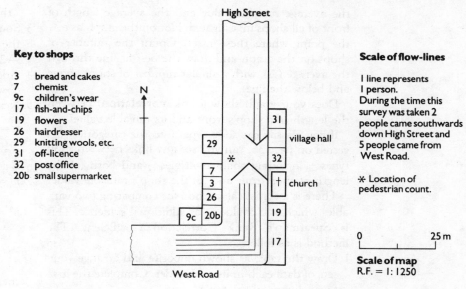

Scale of flow-lines

1 line represents
1 person.
During the time this survey was taken 2 people came southwards down High Street and 5 people came from West Road.

✳ Location of pedestrian count.

0   25 m

Scale of map
R.F. = 1 : 1250

Figure 2 (above)

Figure 3 (left)

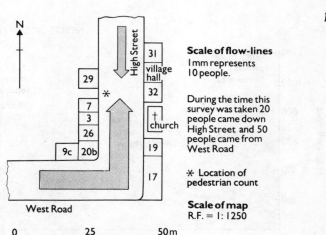

Scale of flow-lines
1 mm represents 10 people.

During the time this survey was taken 20 people came down High Street and 50 people came from West Road

✳ Location of pedestrian count

Scale of map
R.F. = 1 : 1250

0   25   50 m

the average rateable value and the average length of front of all shops investigated. Plot on the graph as a △ the point where these meet. Count the number of shops on the graph and draw the best-fit line through the average (△), with a similar number of shops above and below the line.

Does your graph show a link (**correlation**) between the length of a shop's front and its rateable value?

If you classify the shop types into the categories suggested on page 36, can you see any links between shop types – including chain/multiples – and both (a) the length of shop front and (b) the shop's rateable value?

There is a statistical method for comparing two variables which you could use as additional evidence. This is Spearman's Rank Correlation Coefficient. The method is as follows:

1 Draw the table as shown opposite and arrange your sets of data each in its rank order. Complete the first five columns of the table.

2 Subtract Column 5 (rank order of rateable value), from Column 3 (rank order of length), to complete the 'difference column'.

3 Square the difference, d^2, which means multiplying the number by itself to get rid of negative figures, e.g. $-2 \times -2 = 4$.

4 Add all the figures in the d^2 column to give the sum of d^2 which is written as Σd^2.

5 Next, put your numbers into this formula:

$$r = 1 - \frac{6 \Sigma d^2}{(n^3 - n)}$$

r = the answer
Σd^2 = sum of the square of difference in rank order
n = the number of data used (8 in this example, but it may be more or fewer)
$n^3 = 8 \times 8 \times 8 = 512$

$$r = 1 - \frac{6 \Sigma d^2}{(n^3 - n)}$$

therefore $r = 1 - \dfrac{6 \times 8}{(512 - 8)}$

$$= 1 - \frac{48}{504} = 0.90$$

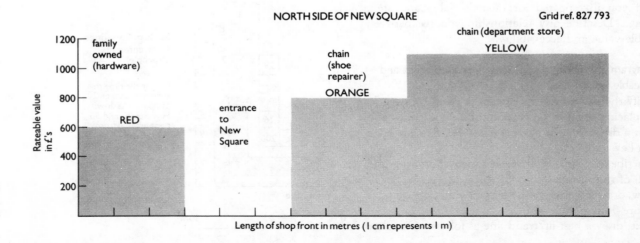

NORTH SIDE OF NEW SQUARE · Grid ref. 827 793

Figure 4 Diagram to show the length of street frontage and reteable value of shops along a street

TYPE/NAME OF SHOP	LENGTH OF SHOP FRONT IN METRES	RANK ORDER OF LENGTH	RATEABLE VALUE IN £'s	RANK ORDER OF RATEABLE VALUE	DIFFERENCE BETWEEN THE RANK ORDERS d	d^2
Supermarket (multiple)	10.0	1	3000	1	0	0
Fashion (multiple)	7.2	2	1900	2	0	0
Betta Shoes (multiple)	6.0	3	1760	3	0	0
D. Lownds (newsagent)	5.5	4	900	5	-1	1
A. Walker (sports equipment)	5.0	5	1000	4	1	1
H. Jesson (butcher)	3.75	6	560	8	-2	4
Dunn (chemist)	3.0	7	725	6	1	1
Sally Lunn (baker)	2.75	8	600	7	1	1
						8

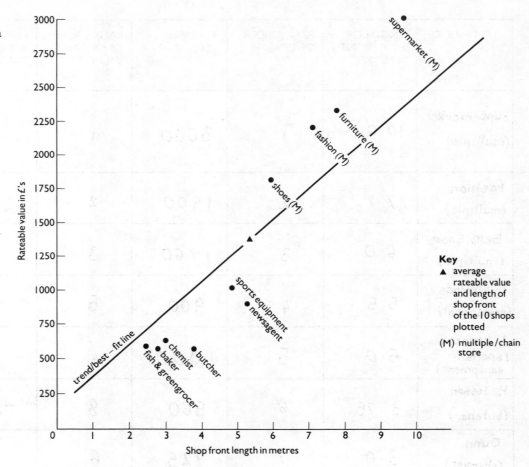

Figure 5 Scattergraph to show the relationship between length of street frontage, rateable value and type of shops

Key
▲ average rateable value and length of shop front of the 10 shops plotted

(M) multiple/chain store

r will range between $+1$ and -1, these showing respectively a perfect positive correlation between the sets of data and a perfect negative correlation. The closer r is to 1 the more certain you may be of a positive relationship.

5 Bar-chart to show the importance of location
Calculate the average values given in answer to each question on the questionnaire. Rank the average figures and draw a bar-chart in rank order to illustrate (a) the features that customers appreciate about location (questions 1 and 2), and (b) other attractions (questions 3 and 4).

6 Sketch-map to show links between accessibility and customer opinion
Calculate the average customer total for each shop. Locate your shops on your map of accessibility and shade them according to high, moderate or low opinion.

Does your map show any relationship between customer opinion and accessibility?

DRAWING CONCLUSIONS
1 From your investigations, describe the types of shops which need to be easily accessible to customers. Give detailed reasons for this.
2 Does your investigation show that many shops which have high rateable values need to have large numbers of customers to make them profitable, and that as a result of this they need to be easily accessible to the public?
3 Describe what you have discovered about the location of small family-owned shops in relation to large chain shops.
4 Does your investigation suggest that certain kinds of shops cluster together in particular areas? Can you suggest why they might do so?

5 Test one or both of these hypotheses:
   (a) 'That chain shops are always located in highly accessible areas of a shopping centre.'
   (b) 'That the rateable value of a shop is not always related to the length of its street frontage.'

FURTHER SUGGESTIONS

1
If you were adviser to the local Planning Committee, in what ways would you improve the accessibility of the shops to customers? Would you demolish some, relocate some, improve pedestrian access, increase public transport or make more car parks? Use knowledge gained in your fieldwork for guidance.

2
Imagine that you are planning the shops to serve a new housing area of about 5000 people. Use the knowledge gained in your fieldwork to help you and locate the shops on a map of scale 1:1250.

4 : To discover the catchment/market area of shops and shopping centres

PREPARATION
How far do you think people are prepared to travel to buy different goods? Arrange this list in the order of distance you think they travel: postage stamps; a dining table and chairs; vegetables; frozen foods; an expensive watch; a new raincoat; a box of chocolates; a set of coloured pencils.

Can you suggest reasons for the order in which you have put them? Is it because of (a) the cost of the good;

SHOPPING QUESTIONNAIRE

NAME OF SCHOOL: _____ DATE: _____

As part of the geography course a study of the shopping services is being made in this area. It would help the study if you would please answer the following questions:

1 What is the name of the town, village or district where you live? _____

2 How often and where do you usually go (name of town or village) for the following:

	Village or town where you shop	How often do you go, e.g., weekly, monthly, yearly?	Distance from home	
			How far do you think you have travelled from home to shop?	
			'perceived' distance	measured distance
(a) Specialised furniture shop or large department store				
(b) Supermarket, hypermarket				
(c) Freezer-centre/specialist deep freeze goods				
(d) Shoe shop				
(e) Post Office				
(f) Shops for Christmas shopping				
REMEMBER TO THANK THE PERSON WHO HAS ANSWERED YOUR QUESTIONS				

Complete this column later using a map and the method explained on page 49.

(b) the frequency with which you would buy it; (c) the ease of access to particular shops?

Make copies of the shopping questionnaire. Ideally, 100 make a good representative sample, and these could easily be printed by microcomputer (see Appendix).

You can discover even more about the catchment area by asking the local newsagent about the area in which newspapers are delivered, and shopkeepers who deliver goods. Write this in your field notebook.

EQUIPMENT
- **Basic fieldkit** including base-map of scale 1:250 000
- **Shopping Questionnaire**

FIELDWORK METHOD
Choose a busy time on a busy shopping day and interview as many people as possible on the streets. People are usually glad to help, but be polite and show them your questionnaire sheets because these explain the

purpose of your survey as a research project. Never ask anyone who appears in a great hurry. Extra interest is gained by completing the questionnaire column headed 'Perceived distance' and, later, measuring on a map the actual difference. You may have some surprises about how big we think our distances are! Add extra or different goods or shops to the questionnaire, but you must be able to give reasons for including them.

PROCESSING THE INFORMATION
Assume that each visit to a shop indicates one purchase.

1 Desire-line maps
Desire-lines show where people travel to shop.

Complete the column headed 'actual distance' on every questionnaire, by measuring accurately the distance along roads from the interviewee's home to the shopping centre, using a piece of string and a pin as in figure 6.

Figure 6 How to measure distance accurately on a map using pin and string

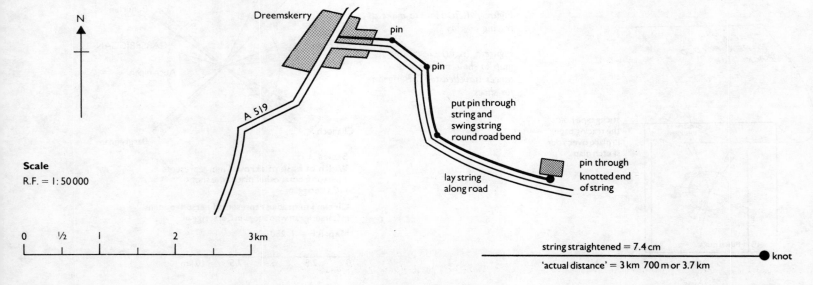

Dreemskerry

pin

pin

put pin through string and swing string round road bend

A 519

lay string along road

pin through knotted end of string

N

Scale
R.F. = 1:50 000

0   ½   1   2   3km

string straightened = 7.4 cm

'actual distance' = 3 km 700 m or 3.7 km

knot

SHOP TYPE	HOME TOWN OR VILLAGE	NUMBER OF PEOPLE SHOPPING IN CARSERIGGAN	FURTHEST DISTANCE TRAVELLED TO CARSERIGGAN
SHOE SHOP	Carseriggan	HHT HHT HHT	
	Achinlech	HHT HHT	
	Bargrennan	III	
	Bendrum	III	
	Challoch	HHT I	
	Kirkcowan	HHT I	
	Upper Ardwall	HHT IIII	7½ km

Choose a sensible scale for the desire-line map. A table like this will show the greatest distance to be drawn and the widest desire-line base and radius of circle.

For this table the 1 250 000 map is big enough for the longest desire-line (7½ km) and for the widest desire-line base (10 mm). Decide whether *you* need a different scale. Instructions for enlarging a map are given on page 3, and if you wish to reduce the scale reverse the instructions.

Decide whether to draw a separate map for each of the goods you have surveyed: you may be able to plot the desire-lines in different colours, or make a **tracing overlay** by placing over your original map as many layers of tracing paper as you need to plot all the goods (figure 7).

Figure 7 (left) How to make a tracing overlay

Figure 8 (right) Desire-line map to show measured distances travelled to Carseriggan for shoes

TRACING PAPER FOLDED BACK

CHRISTMAS SHOPPING

sticky tape holds the tracing paper in place over your sketch map

33 FURNITURE 34

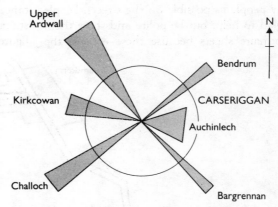

Scales
Width of base of arrow 1 mm represents 1 person from another place who shops in Carseriggan

Circle: 1 mm radius represents 1 person resident in Carseriggan who shops in Carseriggan

Map: R.F. = 1 : 250 000

0   2.5   5   7.5   10 km

Draw a desire-line map for each of the different shopping types completed on the questionnaires (figure 8).

Average the perceived distances to each place. Draw a 'perceived-distance' desire-line map to show how far people *think* they have travelled (figure 9). Place the maps side by side or place one over the other as a tracing overlay. Compare the two maps and describe the differences you see.

2 Map of catchment/market area for all shops investigated

Use a piece of tracing paper and place it in turn over each desire-line map of measured distance. Centre it each time on the shopping centre you are investigating. Draw a line round the bases of the desire-lines on the

maps. Use a different colour for each shop type. In the next diagram different types of lines have been used to show this. Transfer the map onto paper. Finally, on a fresh piece of tracing paper draw the widest catchment area. This is drawn by using the greatest distance travelled to any shop type. Look at figure 10.

Calculate the area in square kilometres of the market area of Carseriggan (see page 96). Suggest reasons for its size.

3 Scattergraph to discover links between number of purchases and distance travelled for shopping

Look at figure 11. For each type of shop in turn calculate the average number of purchases per year and the average distance travelled, using information from the com-

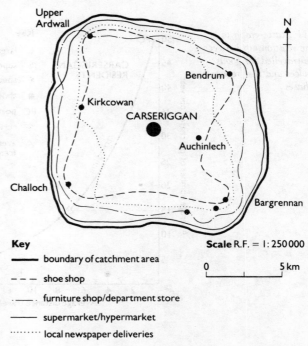

Figure 9 (left) Desire-line map to show perceived distances travelled to Carseriggan for shoes

Figure 10 (right) Catchment/ market area of Carseriggan shopping centre

SHOE SHOPPERS
37 from 'outside'
15 local

Upper Ardwall

Bendrum

N

Kirkcowan

CARSERIGGAN

Auchinlech

Challoch

Bargrennan

Scales
Width of base of arrow: 1 mm represents 1 person from another place who shops in Carseriggan

Circle: 1 mm radius represents 1 person resident in Carseriggan who shops in Carseriggan

Map: R.F. = 1 : 250 000

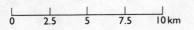

0   2.5   5   7.5   10 km

Key
——— boundary of catchment area
– – – shoe shop
–·–·– furniture shop/department store
——— supermarket/hypermarket
··········· local newspaper deliveries

Scale R.F. = 1 : 250 000

0   5 km

pleted questionnaires. Plot these on a graph.

From all the purchases of every shopping type, calculate the overall average per year. Do the same for the distance travelled to the shops. This is plotted in figure 11 as △. Now draw a line between the two extremes, Post Office and large department store in the diagram, passing through the average. This is the **trend line** and it shows the general trend of information plotted on the graph. Your graph probably looks like figure 11, and you have plotted a **negative correlation**. Think what this term means. The scattergraph on page 46 has a positive correlation.

Describe what your scattergraph tells you about types of goods and how often they are bought and how far people travel to buy them.

Figure 11 Scattergraph to show the relationship between distance travelled for goods and services and the frequency of purchases

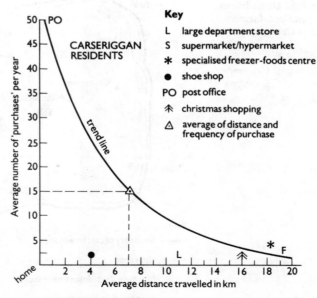

DRAWING CONCLUSIONS

1 Comment on one or more of the following:
  (a) the frequency with which the people interviewed buy different goods;
  (b) the distance the people interviewed travel for different goods;
  (c) the way perceived distance differs from actual measured distance;
  (d) how the size of the catchment/market area alters for different goods.
2 Test one or more of these hypotheses:
  (a) 'That people often perceive distances they travel to be shorter than they are when measured on the map.'
  (b) 'That the catchment/market area for goods bought frequently is smaller than that for goods bought occasionally.'
  (c) 'That people travel further for expensive goods than they do for cheaper goods.'

FURTHER SUGGESTIONS

1

How could you improve shopping services for people living in outlying districts?

2

What would be the advantages and disadvantages of setting up a mobile shop?

INDUSTRY

What does industry mean to you? Here are three main classes of industry with examples of typical employment within each:

Class	Types of employment
Primary/extractive industry	quarrying, forestry work, power station work
Secondary/manufacturing and assembly industry	baking and confectionery, motor vehicle assembly, textile manufacturing
Tertiary/service industry	accountancy, transport driving, security work, nursing, telecommunications

What other types of employment can you think of in each class?

Imagine that you are an industrialist setting up in business. Two important aspects which would influence your choice of site and location of premises would be (a) the availability of employees, and (b) a good transport network. Consider these carefully and make a note of the ways in which they would be of great importance to you. Next consider other aspects such as buildings of particular kinds, the availability of public utilities such as water supply, and links with other firms.

CAUTION
Always carry out your fieldwork in daylight: never be alone: take special care near to roads, railways and canals: keep away from disused and derelict buildings.

FIELDWORK AREAS

Two people can make an interesting and informative investigation of an industrial area of approximately 2 square kilometres. Ideally this should contain at least 10 different industrial establishments. Two smaller industrial areas in contrasting locations may add extra interest: near to contrasting routeways such as a main road and a railway line, or near to a main road and a canal; an old-established industrial part of a town and a part of a new industrial area on the outskirts.

1 : To discover the importance of industry in providing employment

PREPARATION
Prepare your fieldwork investigation in two stages:
1 Make tracings of the area you intend to investigate. First trace a map of scale 1:1250 on which to plot the industries in the area. Also trace a map of scale 1:50 000 and mark on it the industrial area and the surrounding towns and villages where the people who work there may live. Copy the List of Industries on page 55. Each has a number to make plotting easy during your fieldwork. No list could be complete, so add any extra industries which you discover in your area.

INDUSTRY QUESTIONNAIRE

Pupils from _____ School are carrying out a geographical investigation of industry. It would be a great help to our study if you would please complete the following by placing a tick in the appropriate box. (Pupils' names) will call to collect this on _____ (day and date) at _____ (time).

Name of the firm _____ Type of industry _____

1 For how many years has your firm used these premises?

- Under 2 years
- 2 — 4 years
- 5 — 6 years
- 7 — 8 years
- 9 — 10 years
- over 10 years

2 How many people do you employ?

- Under 10
- 10 — 29
- 30 — 99
- 100 — 249
- 250 and over

What percentage of all of your employees is under 30 years of age?

- Under 10
- 10 — 24
- 25 — 49

What is the percentage of male employees?

- 75%
- 50%
- 25%

What percentage of all employees are skilled?

- Under 10%
- 11 — 25%
- 26 — 50%
- 51 — 75%

What is the average distance travelled to work by your employees?

- Under 5 km
- 6 — 10 km
- 11 — 20 km
- over 20 km

Questionnaire (left panel)

How do you cover the main training needs of your employees?
- [ ] by in-service training
- [ ] by external courses such as day-release

3 From what distance do you obtain most of your raw materials?
- [ ] Less than 5 km
- [ ] 5 – 9 km
- [ ] 10 – 24 km
- [ ] 25 – 49 km
- [ ] 50 km and over

At what distance are most of your customers/markets?
- [ ] Less than 10 km
- [ ] 10 – 24 km
- [ ] 25 – 49 km
- [ ] 50 km and over

What methods of transport do you use for most of your transport?
- [ ] Raw materials
- [ ] Finished product
- [ ] Road
- [ ] Rail
- [ ] Canal

Do you own your own containers or lorries?
- [ ] Yes
- [ ] No

LIST OF INDUSTRIES

1. Chemical industry –
   (a) heavy chemicals such as sulphuric acid, oil refining and petrochemicals
   (b) light chemicals such as pharmaceutical products, cosmetics
2. Clothing, dressmaking, tailoring
3. Construction industry, including builders' merchants
4. Craft industries such as basket-making and pottery
5. Electrical goods manufacture such as washing machines and kettles
6. Engineering –
   (a) heavy engineering such as boiler-making, shipbuilding
   (b) light engineering – typewriters, computers, watch-making
7. Food and drink preparation – flour milling, meat processing, brewing, baking and confectionery
8. Furniture manufacture, including fitted kitchens
9. Haulage contractor
10. Joinery – making of doors, window-frames
11. Metal manufacture including steel-making
12. Paper-making
13. Printing and making of photographic equipment
14. Stone-working – monumental masons
15. Textile manufacture
16. 'Warehouse' industries – industrial premises used for the storage of goods before distribution to retail shops

2 Obtain the names and addresses of firms in your chosen area. Write to the manager of each firm enclosing a copy of the industry questionnaire for him to complete. Explain the reason for the questionnaire and suggest a date and approximate time a few days later when you will call to collect it.

EQUIPMENT
- **Basic fieldkit** plus traced maps
- **List of Industries**
- **Industry Questionnaire** — one for the manager of each firm (page 54)

FIELDWORK METHOD
You will have to visit the area twice.

1 First visit
Following your map, walk through the industrial area and identify the ground level use of each industrial establishment. Plot the appropriate number from the List of Industries over each establishment on the map and make a note of the name and address of the firm. Add to your map any industrial premises which have been built or altered since the map was published.

At least twice during the day conduct a traffic count on a main access point from the main road into the industrial area.

2 Second visit
On the day and time you gave, collect the questionnaire from each firm. Try to make sure that it has been completed. You may be able to gain extra information such as the names of the places where the employees live; where the raw materials come from and where the market is for the finished goods.

PROCESSING THE INFORMATION

1 Mapping the types of industry
The industries numbered in the List of Industries may be grouped into categories such as food, textiles and clothing, construction, metals and engineering, chemicals, services. You may alter these six categories according to the area you have investigated, or use the Standard Industrial Classification, published by Her Majesty's Government, which you will find in the reference section of a fairly large public library.

Redraw your map and, choosing a different colour for each category, shade the industrial premises accordingly. Add the key.

Count the number of establishments in each category and then calculate each as a percentage of the total. Describe whether one or two categories appear to be the most numerous. Do your calculations suggest that any industries are particularly important?

2 Mapping the age of firms in the area
Choose a type of shading to represent the different numbers of years that firms have occupied their premises. Shade this information on a separate map or on a tracing overlay (see page 50).

For each category calculate the average number of years that the firm has occupied the premises. Have the most important industries stayed for the longest time?

3 Mapping industrial employment structure
Draw a further map of the industrial area you have investigated. Choosing an appropriate scale, draw over each industrial establishment *either* bar-charts or pie-charts to represent the numbers of employees who are:
    male/female
    under 30 years of age/over 30 years of age
    skilled/unskilled
Give the scale of the bar/pie charts.
Print a letter T over those establishments which have in-service training schemes. Figure 1 shows an example.

Again use your chosen categories of industry and compare your maps and bar-charts or pie-charts. Describe whether there is a relationship between any of the following:

(a) Type of industry and total number of employees.

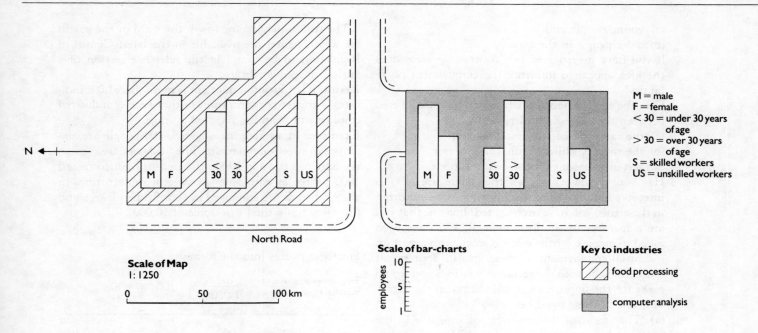

N ←——

M = male
F = female
< 30 = under 30 years
         of age
> 30 = over 30 years
         of age
S = skilled workers
US = unskilled workers

North Road

Scale of Map
1: 1250

0   50   100 km

Scale of bar-charts

employees

10
5
1

Key to industries

▨ food processing

▨ computer analysis

(b) The type of industry and the proportions of male or female labour.

(c) The type of industry and the age-groups of employees.

(d) The type of industry and the proportions of skilled and unskilled labour.

(e) The major employers and in-service training.

4 Assessing the catchment area for employees

For each of the six categories of industry calculate the average distance that employees travel from home to work.

On your tracing of the 1:50 000 scale map take, in turn, the average distance travelled as the radius of a circle centred on the industrial area you have investi-gated. On this scale 1 cm represents ½ km: remember to add this to your map. For each category of industry draw a circle in the same colour used for shading the map of industry types.

Describe the pattern of circles on the map and suggest reasons why they are close together, or why people are prepared to travel further for different types of employment. Has this something to do with skill and pay, or is it related to the surrounding transport network? Are the length of shifts worked important?

DRAWING CONCLUSIONS

1 Describe with illustrations what your fieldwork has revealed about the availability of employment for

Figure 1 Map to show employment structure in industrial units

(a) young people and

(b) older people in the area.

If you have investigated two contrasting areas does the area appear to influence the employment possibilities?

2 Describe any connections which you have discovered between the class of industry and

(a) the ratio of male to female labour;

(b) the ratio of skilled to unskilled labour.

Suggest any reasons for these connections.

3 Has your fieldwork shown that there are labour-intensive industries and machine-intensive industries in the area(s) you have investigated? Imagine that you are a member of the local council, and have been asked to prepare for the other councillors a report on industrial employment in these area(s). Your report must conclude with the recommendations you would make for the improvement of industry in the area.

4 Test one of these hypotheses:

(a) 'That most of the employment available in the area(s) investigated is for skilled labour.'

(b) 'That the most recently established industrial firms are in the tertiary/service class.'

FURTHER SUGGESTION

An accurate way to investigate the degree of concentration of particular industries in your fieldwork area(s) is to calculate the **location quotient** using the following formula:

$$\frac{\dfrac{\text{Number of employees in industry class X in the fieldwork area(s)}}{\text{Number of people employed in all classes of industry in the fieldwork area(s)}} \times 100}{\dfrac{\text{Number employed in industry class X in the region or nation}}{\text{Number employed regionally or nationally in all classes of industry}} \times 100}$$

The region may be the town, the ward or the parish for which figures are available in the latest Census of Population to be found in the reference section of a fairly large public library.

Result: If the location quotient is more than 1.0 it indicates a greater concentration of that type of industrial employment than the regional average.

Example: In an area investigated, 100 people are employed in sweet-manufacture. The fieldwork area lies on the edge of a town in which the Census Returns record 1000 people as employees in sweet-manufacturing. In all, 900 people are employed in your fieldwork area and the town has a total workforce of 10 000.

Put these figures into the formula:

Employees in sweet manufacturing $\qquad \dfrac{100}{1\,000} \times 100 = 10$

Employees in industries of all types $\qquad \dfrac{900}{10\,000} \times 100 = 9$

Location Quotient of Sweet-manufacturing = 1.11

It is accurate to say that sweet-manufacturing is slightly more localised in your fieldwork area than in the town as a whole.

You may calculate the location quotient for each type of industry in the area investigated. Rank the figures and draw a bar-chart with a key ranging from heavy/dark shading for high numbers to light shading for low numbers. Shade the industrial establishments on the map and draw accurate conclusions about their contribution to employment. Do you think that the industrial pattern should be changed to provide a more even balance of types of industry?

2 : To investigate ways in which an industrial area may be improved

The main purpose of industry is to produce goods and/ or to provide services at a profit. 'Factory' is the term given to the special, often purpose-built premises in which people work.

There are many different ways in which an industrial area may be improved: three are considered in the Preparation section.

PREPARATION

First trace the area you intend to investigate from the Ordnance Survey map of scale 1:1250.

Before starting the investigation, plan improvements which you think may be possible. Three examples are given here.

1 Possible improvements to the efficiency of industrial establishments

Factory and warehouse space is usually sold in **industrial units** measured in square metres of floor space. The smallest may be only 30 square metres, and the largest 1000 or 2000 square metres. In newly planned industrial areas the smaller units are sometimes called 'starter units'. In your fieldwork you may be able to pace out the length and width of one or more factories and assess the size of the unit. Practise pacing out distances as described on page 39. Older premises such as mills may be refurbished and divided into units. Discover the cost of buying units of different sizes by contacting the economic development authority within the local council, or estate agents.

Road lighting must comply with standards laid down by the government. Similarly, roads must be of particular widths. Your fieldwork investigation may lead you to feel that firms would benefit from better lighting and a survey of vehicles may convince you that wider roads with better surfaces would also be of benefit. Discover the amount of space needed for loading and unloading of industrial vehicles. Cramped conditions are not efficient.

In order to carry out a traffic survey make at least four copies of the Industrial Traffic Survey sheet on page 61. This one has been partly completed to show you how to fill it in.

2 Improvements to the amenities of the area

All factories must have car parking space. Think of ways in which this could be provided: new units in inner city areas may be built on stilts, with car parks below them. Look at the lay-out of different car parks to discover what you consider to be the most efficient way of using the space. How would you mark out the individual parking spaces?

Public transport may ease pressure on car park space. Discover the frequency of public transport by consulting timetables.

3 Improvements to the industrial landscape

Five different ways in which the landscape may be improved are included in the following scheme. You may need to alter these or add to them in the area(s) you intend to investigate. Make copies of the Industrial Landscape Assessment and Improvement Scheme (page 60) and the Industrial Traffic Survey sheet (page 61).

EQUIPMENT
- **Basic fieldkit** including base-map of scale 1:1250
- **Industrial Traffic Survey sheet** — at least 4 copies
- **Industrial Landscape Assessment and Improvement Scheme** — at least 5 copies
- **List of Industries** — on page 55.

INDUSTRIAL LANDSCAPE ASSESSMENT AND IMPROVEMENT SCHEME

Viewpoint/Grid Reference . . . .

Assessment — Remember that this is an industrial area and not primarily residential

Very pleasant and attractive; no improvements needed ☐

Possible improvements:

More grassed areas, trees and shrubs	External decoration of the buildings	Increase in tidiness	Waste tips need to be hidden from view	Better street lighting needed
☐	☐	☐	☐	☐

FIELDWORK METHOD

First assess the present situation, as described on pages 56 and 59. At the same time record on the map N for units recently built, O for older ones and S for those ones split into smaller units. Devise a key for the presence of solicitors, business consultants, hairdressers, shops and other establishments providing a service.

There is a lot of fieldwork to be done, so be systematic about it. Plan your route carefully so as to collect the maximum amount of information in the minimum of time.

It may well be impracticable to pace out the size of every industrial unit in the area, so use your judgement to choose what appears to be the most usual overall size. Place a tick over the units on the base-map which you intend to measure, and do so when you reach them. The area can be calculated from the Ordnance Survey

DO NOT TRESPASS ON PRIVATE GROUND: Ask permission of a factory official if the loading bay is not visible from the road.

map, but make sure that extensions or sub-divisions of units have not been made since the map was printed. How many storeys are occupied in each unit? Note this on your map.

Measure the width of the roads in the area. *Take great care* when doing so. Note the width on your map together with an assessment of the road surface, which may 'need repair' or 'need more drains to take away water' or be 'excellent'. Twice during the day conduct a traffic survey, perhaps on a main access road and on a smaller road within the industrial area. Record your results on the Industrial Traffic Survey sheet.

As you walk around the area choose locations which give you a good view of the area. Mark the location on the map with this symbol ＼|／ and complete a copy of the Industrial Landscape Assessment and Improvement Scheme by putting √ in the appropriate box or boxes.

Try to discover the loading and unloading facilities at those factories which use very big vehicles. Note on your map whether this was satisfactory or in need of improvement: two or more vehicles queuing at the loading-bay is a waste of valuable time and money.

On different roads pace the distance between lampposts, look at the height of the lights and try to discover whether they are sodium or incandescent. Annotate your map with these details. Is the quality of the lighting satisfactory?

Shade on your base-map the areas of car parks, and mark the location of bus stops like this ● , and bus shelters thus ⬜●⬜ . If you consider a shelter would be an improvement, plot it by the same symbol but use dashed lines around the spot ⌞ ● ⌟ .

INDUSTRIAL TRAFFIC SURVEY

Traffic surveys are being carried out by pupils from. . . . . school.
Vehicles travelling along. . . . .(M.O.T. road number) in the direction of. . . . .

Synchronise your watch with the person counting on the opposite side of the road and signal to each other when to begin. Count for 15 minutes only.

CAUTION: KEEP WELL BACK ON THE PAVEMENT

Count only the vehicles on your side of the road.

LORRY (H.G.V.)	LIGHT VAN	CONTAINER (Record separately from lorry)	TANKER	CAR	BUS OR COACH	BICYCLE
|||		||			ﬀﬀ	++++			

PROCESSING THE INFORMATION

I Mapping the industrial premises to show some possible improvements to their efficiency

Follow the method described on page 56. Shade service establishments distinctively, perhaps in solid black. Make two tracing overlays, one to show the age of the industrial units, perhaps shaded like this

new

old

and the other to show the size of units as a circle the

radius of which is proportional to the area in square metres of each industrial unit. You will know that the area of a circle is πr^2. As π is constant, draw the area of each circle proportional to r^2. Do this by calculating the square root of the area and the answer will be in metres. Choose an appropriate scale for the circles (figure 2).

Are there obvious links between the types of industry and the age of the factory? You may be better able to recognise these if you draw a cumulative bar-chart (see page 103).

2 Annotated diagrams to show industrial traffic and road conditions

The method for drawing a flow-line map of traffic is described on page 43. Use different colours for the different kinds of vehicles counted, and include these in the key.

Annotate your diagram to describe the width of roads and their condition, and add your observations about the area of loading bay in relation to any vehicles you may have seen being used for transport of goods at a factory.

3 Map to show provision of car parks and public transport

On a map of scale 1:1250 shade the areas used as car parks. It may be possible to classify the car parks according to the number of parking spaces, and, if so, use different densities of shading to represent them. Add a key to show this.

From the timetables of public transport draw a flow-line map, choosing the scale of the width of flow line appropriate to the scale of map. It may be significant to represent the types of the transport services in different colours according to different times of day: public transport may be abundant at change-of-shift times, and much less frequent at other times.

Number represented	Square root = radius of circle in mm
100	10
500	22.4
1000	31.6

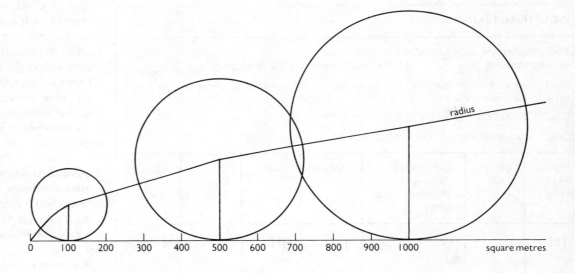

radius

0   100   200   300   400   500   600   700   800   900   1000   square metres

Figure 2 Proportional circles to show floor areas of industrial units

4 Pie-charts to show possible improvements to the industrial landscape

On another map of scale 1:1250, or on a tracing overlay, draw a circle centred on the exact location at which you made a landscape evaluation and considered the required improvements. As in figure 3, divide each circle into five sections, each of which is 72°. Choose a key to the different improvements you consider would make the landscape at each location more attractive. Only shade on each circle the improvements which you think are needed: some viewpoints may have been so pleasing to your eye that you would leave the circle blank.

Also add to the map by means of the symbol suggested for your fieldwork the location of bus shelters if you think that they would be an improvement.

Make lists of two categories of services which you personally consider would be beneficial to the industrial

Grid references of viewpoint: 994 706

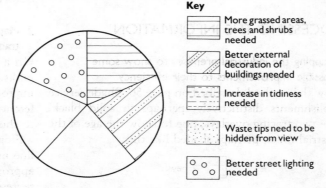

At this viewpoint more grassed areas, trees and shrubs, improvements to external decoration of buildings and better street lighting are considered to be needed.

Key

More grassed areas, trees and shrubs needed

Better external decoration of buildings needed

Increase in tidiness needed

Waste tips need to be hidden from view

Better street lighting needed

Figure 3 Pie-chart to show how the industrial landscape could be improved at this location

area, headed:

(a) Improvements for industrial firms (services could include solicitors, secretarial bureau, accountants in the area);

(b) Improvements for the people who work in the industrial area (e.g. hairdresser, snack-bars, banks, indoor sports area, betting shop, supermarket).

Systematically look at all of your maps, diagrams and written observations, and then write a description of the improvements which you personally would consider desirable. You may use as sub-headings the three kinds of improvement suggested in the introduction on page 59.

DRAWING CONCLUSIONS

1 Write a booklet entitled 'Why modern firms establish themselves in (name of the area investigated)'. Organise the results of your fieldwork into chapters, illustrated by maps and diagrams. Design a cover for the booklet.

2 Describe what your investigations have shown about the good qualities of the industrial area(s) investigated. Recommend ways in which any improvements could be made.

3 In most areas of Great Britain there is an Economic Development Organisation or similar section within the local authority. Imagine that you are a member of such an organisation and are in charge of attracting industrial firms to the industrial area(s) you have investigated. Describe the strong points in favour of firms' coming here.

4 Consider the point-of-view that car parks in an industrial area take up valuable land. Suggest alternatives to the use of cars for journeys between home and work, and ways in which car-park space saved in this way could be used.

5 Test this hypothesis: 'That people who have jobs are concerned with the industrial area as a place of work and do not take notice of the industrial landscape.'

FURTHER SUGGESTIONS

1

Study the rateable value for each of the industrial establishments in the area investigated. Rateable values are available in the Valuation Department of the nearest Town or County Hall. Investigate the public utilities which one or more industrial firm receives in payment of the annual rate. The Economic Development Organisation or similar body at the local Town Hall or County Hall will have such information available.

2

Using journey-time and road congestion as described on pages 13–19, consider whether it would be wiser to encourage greater use of public transport for the journey to work at the industrial area you have investigated.

3

If a river flows through the industrial area you have investigated, take measurements upstream for comparison with those downstream to discover whether there is pollution and of what type(s). Test the pH of the water, the amount of life within it, the amount of sediment (see page 102) and so on.

4

Calculate the area devoted to each of the six categories of industry, and then calculate each as a percentage of the total. Illustrate this as a pie-chart and assess the balance between the different categories. Would you be in favour of altering the balance, and if so why?

3 : To investigate why some industries continue to use old sites and premises

PREPARATION

You may choose to investigate the use of the site of one factory;
a factory which has been split into different industrial units;
a group of factories sited close together.
First trace a map of the premises from an Ordnance Survey map of scale 1:1250 or 1:2500.

Historical maps and documents about the site may be available in a public library or from the local historical society. Older people too may know quite a lot about it and if approached politely will probably be very willing to tell you details. These sources will help you to discover the date of any extensions to the buildings; changes in use; the number of employees at different times and where their homes were; the methods of transport of raw materials to the factory and of finished goods to the market; changes in the source of power used.

One reason for the continued use of the site by industry may be that the rateable value is lower than it would be in a recently built factory. Check these details in the Valuations Department in the nearest Town or County Hall.

You may need to speak to the present owner or manager of the industrial firm(s) to obtain extra and important information, so write to make an appointment at his convenience. Explain that you will not take up much of his time: managers are busy people.

Next look closely at the most recent Ordnance Survey map of scale 1:25 000 or 1:50 000 to discover any reasons why people built industrial premises here in the first place. Look for the following kinds of evidence: a weir or a stream which may have been used to drive a mill wheel; a deeply incised valley with fast-flowing water;

NOTE:
This investigation applies mainly to an area which has continued to have industry on the same site since before 1940.

a canal within easy walking distance for horses – note also the gradients (see page 23) up and down which the horses would have had to walk.

EQUIPMENT
- **Basic fieldkit** and base-maps of the area of scale 1:1250 or 1:2500 and either 1:25 000 or 1:50 000

FIELDWORK METHOD

The investigation may be carried out in stages. First discover as many details as you can by personal observation.

1 Look at the industrial premises themselves, and annotate your large-scale map with any details you consider relevant, for example, date stone, architectural style and building materials used; any evidence of demolition, or refurbishment, including the division of a large building into smaller industrial units: note the number of smaller units; what industry of one or more kinds uses the premises today.

2 Next discover where the homes of the workers and that of the owner were located in the past.

3 Was a source of power a reason for setting up industry here in the past? Has a river been dammed or diverted for a water wheel? Many factories established a long time ago still own the water rights on a nearby river and so save paying a water rate. This will be written in the deeds of the factory and you will have to ask the manager about it. Was steam power later used? A factory chimney will be proof of this. If steam was used, how was the coal brought here and from where?

In the past it was important to have soft water for many industrial processes, although now the water can be softened by adding chemicals. Where is the source of the original water supply and over what types of rocks does it flow? Look at a geological map.

4 Using your small-scale map, 1:25 000 or 1:50 000,

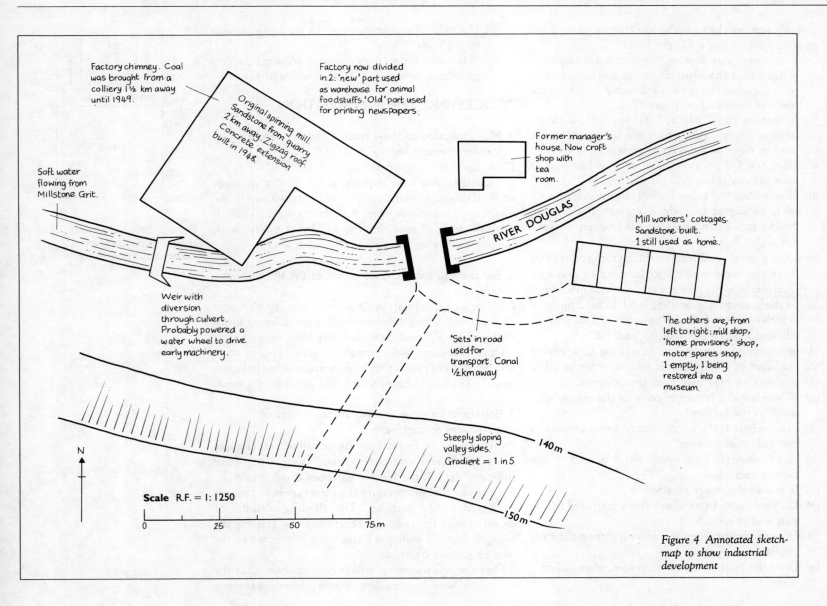

Factory chimney. Coal was brought from a colliery 1½ km away until 1949.

Factory now divided in 2: 'new' part used as warehouse for animal foodstuffs. 'Old' part used for printing newspapers.

Original spinning mill. Sandstone from quarry 2 km away. Zigzag roof. Concrete extension built in 1948.

Former manager's house. Now croft shop with tea room.

Soft water flowing from Millstone Grit.

RIVER DOUGLAS

Mill workers' cottages. Sandstone built. 1 still used as home.

Weir with diversion through culvert. Probably powered a water wheel to drive early machinery.

'Sets' in road used for transport. Canal ½ km away

The others are, from left to right: mill shop, 'home provisions' shop, motor spares shop, 1 empty, 1 being restored into a museum.

Steeply sloping valley sides. Gradient = 1 in 5

140 m

150 m

N

Scale R.F. = 1:1250

0   25   50   75 m

Figure 4 Annotated sketch-map to show industrial development

look for further clues on the site that point to other reasons for building a factory here:

(a) Is the river fast flowing, so that it could turn a water wheel efficiently to power machinery? You may measure the speed of flow by following the method described on pages 97–8.

(b) Is there a canal nearby, perhaps with evidence of an unloading bay, which the factory may have used in the past or even at present?

(c) Does the factory now have or ever has had its own railway siding?

(d) How wide is the valley floor? Has one side or both been excavated to provide enough flat land to build a factory and possibly the original workers' houses?

(e) Does a good road lead to the factory today? Are there the remains of a cobbled road or one with road sets possibly now covered with tar macadam? Is there room for loading and unloading road vehicles today? For the amount of space in an efficient loading-bay refer to page 60.

5 Having obtained permission in writing to speak to the manager of the industrial firm(s), some or all of these questions may help your investigation.

(a) Where are the homes of most of the people who work in the factory?

(b) From where is the water obtained that you use in the industrial process?

(c) Approximately how much water is used in the factory each day?

(d) Is any of the water recycled?

(e) Do you know from where the water used in the past was obtained?

(f) Does the factory own the water rights on the river nearby?

(g) Does the factory own a reservoir, often called a 'lodge'?

(h) Does the firm take measures to prevent pollution of the river?

(i) What advantages does your industrial production gain from being sited in this particular place?

PROCESSING THE INFORMATION

1 Map annotated to show reasons for this choice of location through history

Draw again the large-scale map and, using all the information that you have discovered for factory development at this particular location, add notes to it as in the imaginary example in figure 4. Refer to the 1:25 000 or 1:50 000 scale of map for the height of valley floor, steepness of valley sides and other such details.

2 Bar-chart to show change of use of the site through time

Choose an appropriate scale such as 1 cm to represent 25 years and, using different shading for different kinds of use, draw a cumulative bar-chart as in figure 5.

Draw the chart wide enough to enable you to show any divisions of the factory into separate industrial units and the kinds of industry which take place within them.

3 Bar-charts to show changes in the number of employees through time

Bar-charts are a very good technique to illustrate changes in the numbers of employees through time, if you have sufficient data. If the factory has been divided into different industrial units, count the total number of people employed in the premises. Use shading of different densities over the coloured charts to show the importance of shifts, if shift-work has been important in the past or present (figure 6).

Describe whether your investigations show that the industries have become less or more labour-intensive.

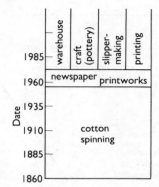

Figure 5 Bar-chart showing changes in the use of an industrial site through time

Key

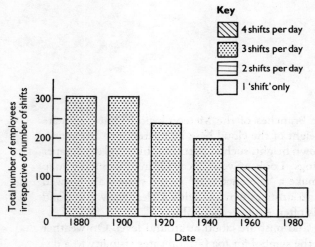

Total number of employees irrespective of number of shifts

Date

▨	4 shifts per day
▧	3 shifts per day
▤	2 shifts per day
□	I 'shift' only

Figure 6 Bar-chart showing changes in the numbers of employees and the changing shift organisation

Express this as the number of employees per square metre of factory. Remember that the factory may have more than one storey.

Describe any links between the labour intensiveness and changes in the type of industry. Or do you think that the labour intensiveness has altered with improvements in industrial techniques?

4 Map of the catchment area for workers

Use different colours to represent different dates and either draw desire-lines, as described on page 50 or draw concentric circles as described on page 8, to show where the workers have lived at different times. Add a key to the colours used.

Describe differences through time and suggest reasons based on what you have discovered about transport methods.

DRAWING CONCLUSIONS

1 Using the facts you have discovered, explain which factors have been important to the location of industry on this site at different periods of time.

2 Imagine that you have been asked to give a guided tour to demonstrate to a group of geographers industrial change in the location you have investigated. Plan the way in which you would set about doing this and write notes on each aspect which you would include in your tour.

3 Compile a booklet about the facts you have discovered: divide it into different chapters according either to time or to changes in types of industry.

4 Describe what your investigations have shown about the reasons why industry has continued to occupy this location.

5 Test one of these hypotheses:

(a) 'That a historical investigation of a particular location is essential to the understanding of geographical inertia at the present time.'

(b) 'That the location of industry at the present time can be fully understood without any reference to the past.'

FURTHER SUGGESTION

Conduct a similar investigation in an industrial location run by a conservation group. Write first to the organiser to gain permission to do so, and, when you have completed both investigations, give your own opinions as to why industry has continued to be profitable in the first location, and yet conservationists have taken over and preserved the second industrial location.

You may conclude by giving your own views on the importance for present and future generations of creating conservation areas.

WEATHER

When not 'on top of the world' some people describe themselves as 'feeling under the weather' and the weather is a well-proven way of opening conversation, so it seems to be very important to most of us. It does affect our lives and sometimes the way we earn our living: farming, umbrella-manufacturing, the clothes we wear, arrivals and departures at airports, sports, gardening. Make a list of all the ways in which weather affects us. Also, have you noticed which aspects of the weather people talk about most, and the ways in which people differ in their opinion about the weather on the same day?

Expensive and sophisticated equipment can be bought to discover various aspects of the weather and your school may have its own weather station. In any case, with a little practice it is easy to make your own weather map and to forecast the weather in the forthcoming hours and days.

USEFUL TECHNIQUES

1 How to recognise clouds and estimate visibility
Different kinds of cloud are called by Latin names. Find out what each name means. Learn to recognise the shape of the main types of cloud: most reference books show pictures of cirrus, stratus, cumulus and combinations of these. The bases of clouds begin at different heights. When people sometimes remark that 'the sky is high' they really mean that the cloud base is high and it is unlikely to rain.

The branches of the Meteorological Office estimate the height of the cloud base by reference to landmarks of known height, such as particular hills and sky scraper buildings. Look at your local Ordnance Survey map and make a 'reference map' in the same way. Viewed from an upstairs window with a clear view the cloud base is often easily recognisable.

Fog and mist are cloud at ground level. On weather maps the symbol for fog ($\equiv$) indicates visibility to a distance of 1 km and the symbol for mist ($=$) indicates visibility to within 1 to 2 km. The Meteorological Office gives fog warnings for different purposes – for farmers, fishermen, air-traffic controllers, motorists, railways and so on. Warnings of 'airfield fog' are given if the shape of a known object is not recognisable at distances over 1000 m (1 km). Fog warnings for motorists are given only if an object is unrecognisable at distances greater than 200 m. An airline pilot needs to see clearly for a much greater distance than a motorist does, because he is travelling much faster.

You can try the Meteorological Office's method for yourself. Find on the Ordnance Survey map of your area objects such as church spires or multistorey buildings that are 1000 m and 200 m distant from your observation point and visible on a clear day. If you can see only the 200 m distant object, 'airfield fog' exists; if you can see neither object, then 'motorists' fog' conditions exist at that time. Draw a map similar to figure 1 and call it a **visibility map**.

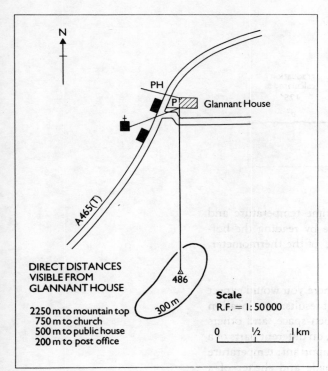

Figure 1 Visibility map

DIRECT DISTANCES VISIBLE FROM GLANNANT HOUSE

2250 m to mountain top
750 m to church
500 m to public house
200 m to post office

Scale
R.F. = 1 : 50 000

0 ½ 1 km

2 How to estimate the amount of cloud cover

The amount of sky which is covered by cloud is measured in eighths. The Greek word **okta** is used to describe the amount of cloud cover.

Make a **cloud cover recorder** using a cardboard tube 4 or 5 cm diameter and 20 cm long (figure 2).

Hold the tube vertically and, looking through it with one eye, assess the amount of sky which is covered. Record this in oktas and later complete your recording sheet with the official symbol. (Look up the cloud cover symbols in figure 10 on page 76.)

embroidery thread divides the tube-end into eighths (oktas)

45° angle

Figure 2 Cloud cover recorder

3 How to measure air pressure and wind

Use an aneroid barometer to measure the air pressure in millibars. Compare results day by day and judge whether the pressure is rising, falling or remaining fairly constant. Note that as you climb uphill there is less atmosphere above to press down upon you and the pressure drops by 11 millibars for every 100 m. The pressure shown on maps is usually converted to 'sea level pressure'.

Wind direction and speed must be assessed in as open a space as possible. It is useful to dig a four-sided stake into the ground so that one side faces north, another west and the others south and east. Mark the compass direction on each side. Fasten a piece of coloured tape or ribbon onto the top and this will enable you to record the direction from which the wind is blowing.

Throughout the world wind speed is recorded in knots, except in the Soviet Union where it is measured in metres per second. To measure wind speed accurately

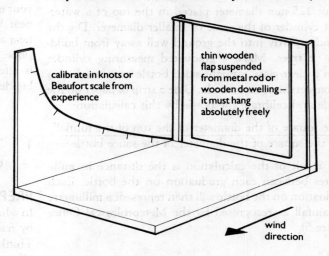

calibrate in knots or Beaufort scale from experience

thin wooden flap suspended from metal rod or wooden dowelling – it must hang absolutely freely

wind direction

Figure 3 How to make an anemometer

you need an anemometer. These are very expensive to buy but you can make one as shown in figure 3 or use the Beaufort Scale.

On a weather map wind is recorded as an arrow, and the speed as tail-feathers on the arrow (figure 4).

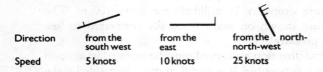

Direction	from the south west	from the east	from the north-north-west
Speed	5 knots	10 knots	25 knots

Figure 4 Symbols for wind direction and speed

4 How to measure precipitation

Rain is a liquid. Officially it is recorded in millimetres. Hail, snow and sleet are also precipitation and must be melted before they are recorded. Snow melts down to approximately 1/10 of its depth as water.

You can easily make a rain gauge from a funnel of about 125 mm diameter placed in the top of a water-tight cylinder of the same or smaller diameter. Dig the cylinder partly into the ground well away from buildings or trees. Make a graduated measuring cylinder from a clear-glass, straight-sided bottle or jar such as a Worcestershire sauce bottle. Glue a strip of paper up the bottle and calibrate the bottle by this calculation:

$$\frac{\text{the square of the diameter of the top of the funnel}}{\text{the square of the diameter of the sauce bottle}}$$

The result of the calculation is the distance in millimetres between each graduation on the bottle. Each graduation on the bottle will then represent a millimetre of rainfall as recognised by the Meteorological Office (figure 5).

5 How to record temperature

If you have a maximum-and-minimum thermometer you can discover the maximum daytime temperature and minimum night-time temperature by reading the bottom of the metal tab in each 'side' of the thermometer.

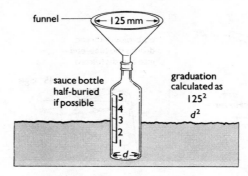

Figure 5 How to make a rain gauge

FIELDWORK AREAS

Choose a number of locations where you would expect your equipment to record different results: try a location near buildings, another in an open space, and others near a hedge or fence, under trees, on different parts of a slope. The choice of location is important: temperature is affected by the amount of shade and shelter of a building; wind and rainfall by the degree of exposure.

I : To examine the effect of buildings and other features upon weather conditions

PREPARATION

In what ways are wind, temperature and rainfall affected by features such as buildings, walls, hedges and trees? Think how you would devise ways of measuring the effects upon the weather conditions. You may have to adapt the suggestions here because the size and shape of

WEATHER RECORDING SHEET					
DATE:					
		TIME 1: **0900h**	TIME 2: **1030h**	TIME 3: **1300h**	TIME 4: **1600h**
LOCATION 1:	TEMPERATURE	19 °c			
	WIND DIRECTION	SW			
	WIND FORCE	Fluttering			
	RAINFALL	/			
	ANY OTHER WEATHER CONDITIONS	Cumulus clouds			
LOCATION 2:	TEMPERATURE	21 °c			
	WIND DIRECTION	/			
	WIND FORCE	limp			
	RAINFALL	/			
	ANY OTHER WEATHER CONDITIONS	Cumulus clouds			
LOCATION 3:	TEMPERATURE	19 °c			
	WIND DIRECTION	SW			
	WIND FORCE	Fluttering			
	RAINFALL	/			
	ANY OTHER WEATHER CONDITIONS	Cumulus clouds			

school buildings and the lay-out of the grounds vary.

Locate each point at which you will take recordings on an Ordnance Survey map of scale 1:1250 or on a plan of the school. You may wish to do further suggestion No. 1 so look at the instructions on page 73. Make a copy of the Weather Recording Sheet (page 71).

EQUIPMENT:

- **Instruments:** The thermometers and bias binding must be placed at the same height at each location. Posts may already be available – gate post, goal post, tree trunk – but make sure that the instruments will not be damaged during school activities.
- **Weather Recording Sheets**

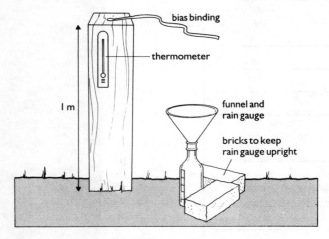

Figure 6 Home-made weather instruments

FIELDWORK METHOD

Take readings as many times as possible, either at set intervals or at random throughout the day. Take the readings at the different locations as close together in time as possible.

PRECAUTIONS

1 **Be as accurate as possible every time you take a reading and record it.**
2 **If the bias binding is limp it will be almost impossible to record the direction from which the wind is blowing.**
3 *Either* **empty the rain gauge completely after each reading** *or* **– and this makes reading of the amount easier – remember to deduct the previous recorded amount.**
4 **Collect in all instruments at the end of the day.**

If using bias binding, devise a system of comparison of wind force perhaps:

'bias binding limp'
'bias binding fluttering'
'bias binding extended'.

You may be able to convert these to approximate to the Beaufort Force and even to wind speed in knots.

PROCESSING THE INFORMATION

1 Graphs of temperature and rainfall

Draw graphs as in figure 7, to show your recordings. Make the scale big enough to show any variations.

Describe any variations in temperature and rainfall which you see between the different locations and times of recordings. Can you suggest reasons for these? Make a note of them.

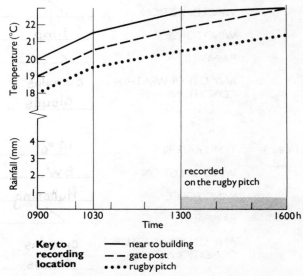

Figure 7 Graphs of weather recordings in the school grounds

2 Illustration of wind direction and wind force

For each location and time draw an arrow to show the wind direction recorded (figure 8). Add to the arrow a symbol to show the wind force. Here is a suggestion:

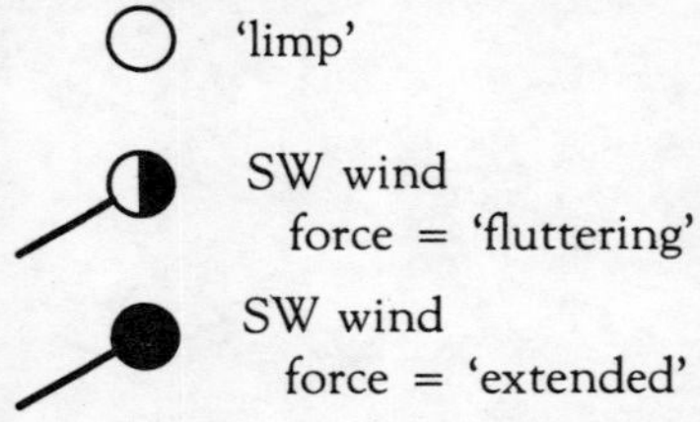

○ 'limp'

SW wind force = 'fluttering'

SW wind force = 'extended'

Note that 'limp' does not have an arrow because, in this condition, it is almost impossible to tell the wind direction.

Describe any variations which your illustration shows. Suggest how the location of the instruments may have affected the direction and force.

3 Map annotated to show and explain variations in weather conditions in the school grounds

For each time of recording copy the large-scale map used in your preparation and plot the recordings at each location marked. Add notes to explain variations in the conditions. Your map may look something like figure 9.

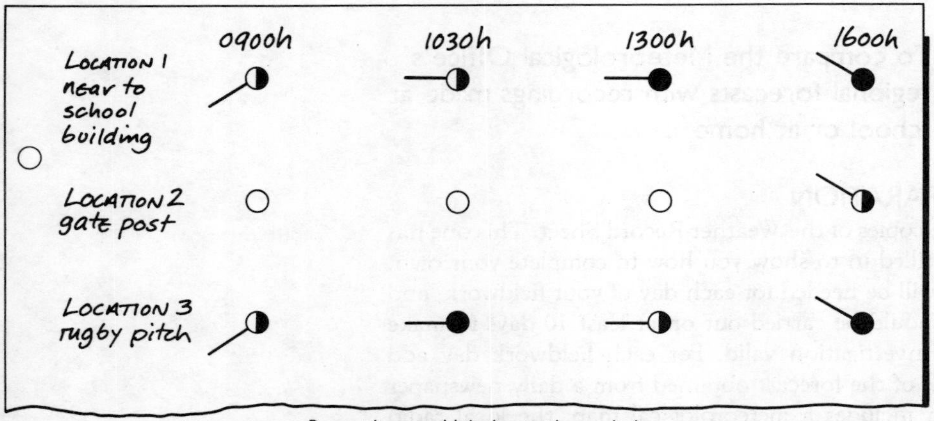

Figure 8 Simple symbols to record wind conditions

Location 1 near to school building

Location 2 gate post

Location 3 rugby pitch

0900h   1030h   1300h   1600h

Remember to add the key to the symbols

Compare your maps and describe any patterns in weather conditions which seem to be related to the location of the instruments. Suggest reasons for these patterns.

DRAWING CONCLUSIONS

1 Describe the weather conditions at each location, recorded at different times, and suggest how the buildings and other features have affected them.

2 If you were asked to set up *one* weather station in the school grounds, describe with reasons which location you would choose to obtain the most accurate readings.

3 Consider ways in which the weather would affect your decisions if you were asked to plan one or more of the following:

(a) an extension to the school building;
(b) a detached house with gardens on all four sides;
(c) a cricket pitch or tennis court;
(d) a market garden of approximately ½ hectare in size.

What effects would your finished piece of work have upon the local climate? Remember from your fieldwork the effects that buildings have on such weather conditions as wind force and direction, and temperature.

4 Test this hypothesis:

'That wind is the weather condition most affected by buildings.'

FURTHER SUGGESTIONS

1

Compare the temperature and wind force and direction close to ground level with those at a higher level. On each post chosen place a second thermometer as close to the ground as possible and attach a second piece of

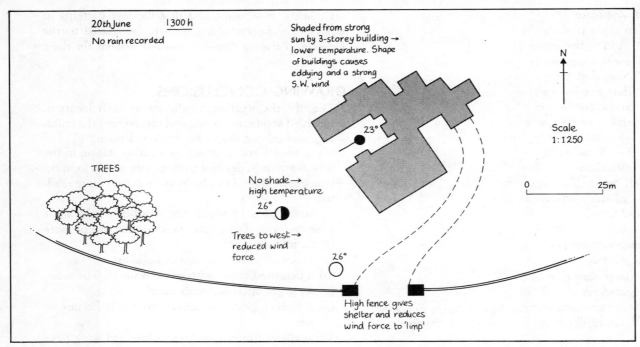

Figure 9 Map to show and explain variations in weather conditions in the school grounds

Within the figure:

20th June   1300 h
No rain recorded

Shaded from strong sun by 3-storey building → lower temperature. Shape of buildings causes eddying and a strong S.W. wind

TREES

No shade → high temperature
26°

Trees to west → reduced wind force

23°

26°

High fence gives shelter and reduces wind force to 'limp'

N

Scale
1:1250

0   25m

---

bias binding about 30 cm above the ground. Record these as 'ground level' readings. Compare the two sets of recordings and consider how valuable they might be for farmers, including market gardeners and horticulturalists, Parks and Gardens Departments and people who have flower and/or vegetable gardens.

2

Investigate the effect of aspect by placing a thermometer on each side of a square post in an exposed place positioned with sides facing north, south, east and west. On a sunny day take readings at intervals and compare them. Suggest from your results why, for accuracy, thermometers must be kept in a Stevenson Screen.

2 : To compare the Meteorological Office's regional forecasts with recordings made at school or at home

PREPARATION

Make copies of the Weather Record Sheet. This one has been filled in to show you how to complete your own. One will be needed for each day of your fieldwork, and this should be carried out on at least 10 days to make your investigation valid. For each fieldwork day add details of the forecast obtained from a daily newspaper which includes a meteorological map, the local radio station, the local television channel, the telephone

WEATHER RECORD SHEET: FORECAST AND OBSERVED

DATE: September 15		TIME OF OBSERVATIONS: **0900h**
	FORECAST	OBSERVED
PRECIPITATION AMOUNT	heavy	6mm
TYPE	rain	rain and hail
TIME OF PRECIPITATION	late afternoon	1400h – 1530h
AMOUNT OF CLOUD COVER	cloudy after midday	◖ 6 oktas
CLOUD TYPE	/	big cumulus
HOURS OF SUNSHINE	4h – reported in newspaper on following day	about 2hours in the morning
TEMPERATURE DAY	20°c	maximum temp. 21°c
NIGHT	8°c	minimum temp 6°c
WIND SPEED	8 knots	5 knots
WIND DIRECTION	S.E.	S.S.E
OTHER WEATHER CONDITIONS	thunderstorms possible in the afternoon	

recorded information service: 'Weather Forecast', or the local Weather Centre.

EQUIPMENT
- **Weather recording instruments**
- **1 copy of the Weather Record Sheet for each day's fieldwork**

FIELDWORK METHOD
Carry out your observations in the same way each time. 0900 h is a good time to take readings, but notice the times during the day when it rains, and estimate the hours of sunshine between the times of getting up and going to bed. Dawn to dusk is obviously the most accurate period of time but in summer it is not always practicable!

Your own observations of rainfall and of maximum and minimum temperatures will be those for the previous 24 hours, so pay attention to the date on the Weather Record Sheet when you record the observations. You may discover from the newspaper the hours of sunshine for the previous day.

PROCESSING THE INFORMATION

1 Mapping the information
Draw two maps of your local region side by side: the first to show the previous day's forecast and the second to show the weather you observed.

You will interest the whole school if you mount these on a magnetic sheet. Weather symbols which can be moved each day as necessary can be made from paper backed with magnetic tape, bought from a do-it-yourself shop. Magnetic tape is expensive but it does go a long way. An equally attractive and interesting display could be made on paper or on a blackboard.

Copy two or more isobars and a front from the news-paper weather map onto the forecast map. You will need the symbols shown in figure 10.

Figure 11 gives some optional symbols, or you may devise your own.

It is vital that all of your observations are made and recorded with great care. Inaccurate work at any stage will make the whole investigation worth nothing.

Figure 10 *Weather symbols for use on a large display map*

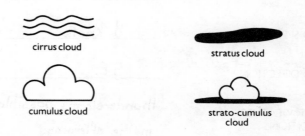

Figure 11

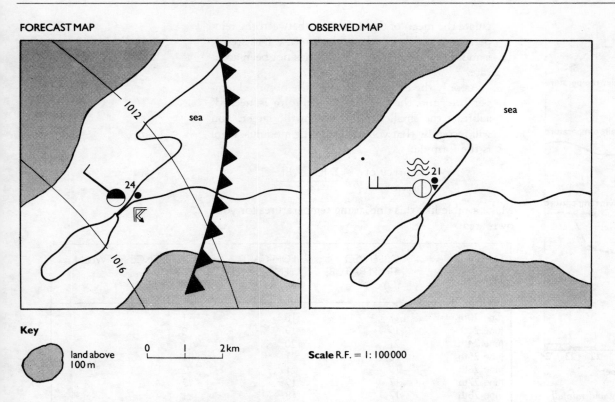

FORECAST MAP

OBSERVED MAP

1012

sea

1016

24

sea

21

N

Figure 12 Forecast and observed weather maps of a local area

Key

land above 100 m

0   1   2 km

Scale R.F. = 1 : 100 000

Your maps will look something like figure 12. Also remember to add a key to the symbols.

2 Temperature and precipitation graphs

For ten or more days draw a line graph of temperatures recorded and bar-charts of precipitation recorded as in figure 13. If you have used a maximum-and-minimum thermometer you may show both of these and also calculate the mean temperature for each 24 hour period.

Maximum temperature at noon, and possibly a nighttime temperature, may be the only ones forecast. Use the same scale as for the graph of observed temperatures

and either draw graphs of forecast temperature beside those of observed weather or make a tracing overlay.

3 Comparing the forecast temperatures with those observed

There are several ways in which you can compare the forecast and observed values, but you will have to give your own assessment of the accuracy of the forecasts. Remember that it would be absolutely unfair and inaccurate to base upon this one aspect of the weather your opinion of the whole of the work of the Meteorological Office in producing regional forecasts.

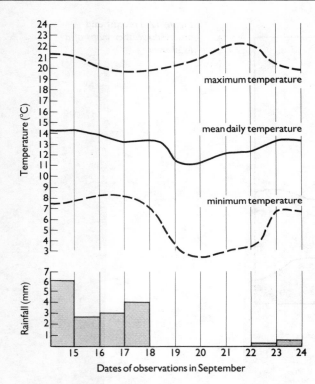

Figure 13 Graph to show observed temperature and rainfall

(a) Bar-charts: Shade the observed temperature in one colour and the forecast in another. Leave a space between the days.

(b) Scattergraph: See page 46 for how to draw a scattergraph. Use the same scale for both axes and, after plotting the temperatures, assess how close the points are to the line $x = y$ (the line through all the points where observed temperature equals forecast temperature). The closer they are the more accurate is the forecast.

(c) Mathematical test: As in the example below, cal-culate the mean of the differences between the temperatures you observed and the forecast. If the result is more than 2 then the forecast has not been accurate.

As only the *difference* between the observed temperature and the forecast temperature is needed, subtract the smaller number from the larger. You will recognise that you are using the modulus. Here is the formula:

$$\text{accuracy of forecast} = \frac{\Sigma\,|O - F|}{n}$$

Make a table like this one, using temperatures for your own area:

DATE	OBSERVED TEMPERATURE (O)	FORECAST TEMPERATURE (F)	DIFFERENCE BETWEEN O AND F (MODULUS)
June 20th	17	18	1
June 21st	19	19	0
June 24th	21	20	1
June 25th	20	21	1
June 26th	19	21	2
June 27th	17	19	2
June 28th	17	18	1
July 1st	20	18	2
July 2nd	20	19	1
July 3rd	22	21	1
SUM OF DIFFERENCES			12

Mean of the sum of the differences $= \dfrac{12}{10} = 1.2$

Conclusion: The Meteorological Office's forecasts were accurate.

DRAWING CONCLUSIONS

1 Describe what your investigation has shown about the accuracy, applied to a small area, of regional forecasting by the Meteorological Office.
2 Describe what types of instruments you would like to enable you to make a more detailed observation of weather conditions. Devise ways of making some.
3 Suggest with reasons where you would locate other weather stations within the area to enable forecasts to be made.
4 Test this hypothesis:
'That the Meteorological Office's forecasts for (name of your area) for the period (date) to (date) were accurate.'

FURTHER SUGGESTIONS

I

Draw a map, similar to the one suggested on page 77, of Western Europe to include the British Isles. By plotting the daily weather maps copied from a newspaper, forecast the weather at school for the next few days. See how accurate your own forecasts are; with practise they will soon become reliable.

2

Compare the weather you observe with details given on weather maps published in the newspapers. Suggest reasons for the weather from the position of the fronts, isobars and wind directions shown.

3 : To investigate the importance of weather in people's lives

PREPARATION

Make a diary for a week including Saturday and Sunday, setting it out with enough space to record details as shown (see page 80).

EQUIPMENT

- **Weather Diary**
- **Weather recording instruments**
- **Newspaper weather reports**
- **Weather Questionnaire**, at least 20 copies.

FIELDWORK METHOD

I Weather Diary

Keep the Weather Diary for a week. It is important to complete it each day in the order in which it is set out because if, for example, you know the temperature figure, you may be tempted to convince yourself that the day is cold or hot! Examples of the sort of comments you might make are shown.

2 Weather Questionnaire

Using the Weather Questionnaire, interview at least 20 people. To avoid a biased opinion, never interview someone who has overheard another interview taking place.

Complete a questionnaire for yourself and if possible interview 5 adults, and 5 people in each year in school. You could then add 'age' to the questionnaire, and later assess whether it has any bearing upon the answers.

This questionnaire has been planned to allow you to process the results by computer and so save time. When the answer to a question is already written put a ring around the answer given by the interviewee, like this:

Question: Did it rain last week? *Answer:* (Yes)/No. This shows that the interviewee thought it had rained last week.

WEATHER DIARY

Day and date: _____

1. MY OWN IMPRESSIONS OF THE WEATHER:
   dull, miserable and drizzling

2. ANY SPECIAL CLOTHES I WORE BECAUSE OF THE WEATHER:
   a mac

3. THE EFFECT OF THE WEATHER UPON MY ACTIVITIES:
   I stayed in at break

4. WEATHER RECORDINGS:

   Temperature: _____

   Precipitation: Amount _____ type _____

   Wind direction: _____

   Wind speed: _____

   Amount of cloud cover: _____

   Hours of sunshine: _____

   Atmospheric pressure: _____

WEATHER QUESTIONNAIRE

1 Did it rain last week? Yes / No

2 Do you remember on which day or days it rained? Sun. / Mon. / Tues. / Wed. / Thurs. / Fri. / Sat.

3 (a) At any time in the week did the rainfall make you wear any special clothing? Yes / No

   (b) If 'YES' ask 'In what way?' _____

4 (a) At any time in the week did the temperature make you wear any special clothing? EXPLAIN IF NECESSARY: Was it too hot or too cold for what you normally wear at this time of year? Yes / No

   (b) If 'YES' ask 'In what way?' _____

5 (a) Did the weather affect what you did on either Saturday or Sunday? Yes / No

   (b) If 'YES' ask 'In what way?' _____

6 Can you describe the weather on any day last week? Day: _____ Description: _____

PROCESSING THE INFORMATION

1 **Comparison between personal impressions and weather recorded**

Use your diary to complete a copy of the table opposite.
Put a tick in the column against each weather condition

which was your own impression (I) and/or was recorded by instruments or the newspaper report (R). 'Rain' and 'sun' have been completed to show you how to do it.

R is always correct; therefore, the more often I agrees with R the more accurate your impressions were. Wherever I agrees with R give yourself a score of 1. The maximum score is 70 (10 different weather conditions on 7 different days).

Calculate your score as a percentage of 70 to find out how accurate your impressions were.

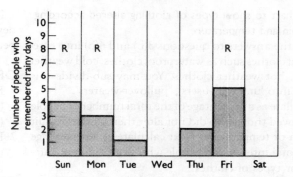

Figure 14 Bar-chart showing the accuracy of people's perception of the days with rain

WEATHER CONDITION	SUN		MON		TUES		WED		THU		FRI		SAT	
	I	R	I	R	I	R	I	R	I	R	I	R	I	R
Rain	✓	✓	–	✓	–	–	–	–	–	–	✓	✓	–	–
Sun	–	–	–	✓	✓	✓	✓	✓	–	✓	–	–	✓	✓
Cold														
Hot														
Windy														
Foggy														
Snow														
Hail														
Thunder														
Frost														

2 Bar-chart to compare remembered rainy days with actual rainy days

Use the answers to question 2 of the questionnaire to show the number of people who remembered the days on which it rained. Use the recorded weather in your Weather Diary to mark with a letter R the days on which it actually rained (figure 14).

As further evidence, you may calculate as a percentage the number of people who remember correctly. Describe what your bar-chart and calculation show about how accurately people notice the weather.

3 Bar-charts to show how many people altered their clothing because of the weather

Draw bar-charts side by side to illustrate the number of 'Yes' and 'No' answers to questions 3 and 4. Use the same scale for both bar-charts.

1 Calculate the percentage of people who altered their clothing because of rain.
2 Calculate the percentage of people who altered their clothing because of temperature.
3 Describe whether you consider rain or temperature to have the greater influence upon people's clothing.

4 Pie-chart to show types of clothing altered according to rain and temperature

Group the answers to questions 3(b) and 4(b) into categories of clothes such as waterproof clothes, cold weather clothes, hot weather clothes. You may sub-divide this further into 'umbrella-users', 'pullover-wearers'.

Calculate as a percentage of the total number of people interviewed those who did not alter their clothes to suit the rain or temperature. Next calculate as a percentage of the total interviewed people who wore different categories or types of clothes.

Draw a pie-chart to illustrate this like the one on page 9. 3.6° of the circle represents 1%. Remember to add a key. Describe what your pie-chart shows.

5 Pie-chart to show the effect of weather on weekend activities

Use the answers to question 5 to calculate as a percentage of the total number of people interviewed those whose activities were not affected. Group the answers to 5(b) into categories. Illustrate these on a pie-chart, and add a key.

Look up in your Weather Diary what weather conditions were recorded on Saturday and Sunday and write these beside the pie-chart. Suggest whether or not the weather did affect people's activities. Was this as a result of an unexpected change in the weather?

6 Comparison between remembered weather and recorded weather

To illustrate answers to question 6 construct a table like the one on page 81 but on a scale big enough to include all the people you interviewed. Place peoples' 'remembered weather' under column I.

Calculate the mathematical formula given and describe what is shown by both the table and the mathematical result. Memories sometimes seem very short!

If you have taken a sample of different age-groups, devise a method a correlating age with memory. Do people become more or less aware of weather with age?

DRAWING CONCLUSIONS

1 From your Weather Diary assess
   (a) the accuracy of your impressions of the weather;
   (b) the effect which the weather had upon you.
2 From your questionnaires describe
   (a) how much people notice the weather;
   (b) what effect it has upon them.
3 To which groups of people is the weather of great importance? Suggest reasons why these people would remember very clearly the recent pattern of weather.
4 Test one of these hypotheses:
   (a) 'That people who work mostly indoors do not need to take notice of the weather.'
   (b) 'That people's leisure time is more affected by weather than time spent working.'

FURTHER SUGGESTIONS

I

Refer to the chapters on 'Shops and Shopping' (pages 34–52) and 'Outdoor Leisure Area' (pages 5–19). Bearing in mind the assessment you have made of the importance of weather to people, suggest plans you would make for shopping areas and recreation facilities.

2

Has your investigation led you to believe that central heating, air conditioning, double glazing and tinted glass should be used more widely? Consider the advantages and disadvantages, including cost, of installing such 'weather protection' into public and private buildings and public and private transport.

SOILS

Prehistoric man was able to detect the fertility of the soil for his farming by recognising indicator plants: succulents indicate sandy soil; heather an acid, peaty soil; willow trees water-logged, gley soil. What do sea-pinks indicate? Do you know of any other indicator plants?

Have you ever thought what soil really is? Some people define it as 'the material in which plants grow'. There are many different kinds of soil, such as clay soil and limy soil. Can you think of others?

Some people change the nature of the soil in the course of their work. Farmers, gardeners and groundsmen may alter the soil's texture, acidity and plant food. Why do they do so? If you were a farmer or a gardener, what you could grow would depend upon the texture of the soil and also on its acidity, or pH value.

pH is a logarithmic measure of the concentration of the hydrogen ions in the soil. If the pH value is less than 6.5–7 the soil is acid, and if it is more the soil is alkaline. Plants absorb nutrients dissolved in the soil water. The pH influences the solubility of the nutrients and therefore the fertility of the soil.

If you had a vegetable garden here are some crops you could grow in soils of different pH values:

pH 5–6	pH 6.5–7.0	pH 6.5–7.5
potatoes	broad beans	carrots
rhubarb	peas	cauliflowers
	cabbages	

Discover from a gardening book the kinds of shrubs, heathers and flowers which grow best in soils of particular pH values.

Texture affects the drainage, the amount of air within the soil and the ease of cultivation. Below are some of the advantages and disadvantages of two kinds of texture: add your own ideas to the lists.

SANDY SOILS
ADVANTAGES
- 'Light' and easy to cultivate
- Warm quickly in spring and can, therefore, be cultivated early

DISADVANTAGES
- Contain few nutrients and need to be fertilized often
- Easily eroded by wind
- Drain very easily

CLAY SOILS
ADVANTAGES
- Retain water for a long time, which is helpful during dry weather
- Contain many nutrients

DISADVANTAGES
- 'Heavy' and difficult to cultivate

FIELDWORK AREAS
A complete soil profile may be seen in a river bank or in a cutting such as for roadworks. If not, you will either

For soil investigations on private land it may be necessary to request permission before beginning. It is vitally important that you should not spoil the landscape in any way or leave behind holes which might be dangerous to people or to animals.

have to use a soil auger – the Swedish 'walking stick' type which gives a core is preferable to the screw type – or use a small spade to dig a hole two spade-widths square. The hole can be filled in afterwards to leave little trace of disturbance.

Investigations of topsoil, down to a depth of 15 cm, can be very interesting. If you decide to investigate two or more soils, try to choose contrasting sites such as:
on different parts of a slope;
beneath different types of vegetation – woodland and meadowland;
topsoil from a rose bed or a playing field.

PREPARATION

It is wise to become familiar with soil colours and tex-tures, and testing for pH value, before beginning your fieldwork, so collect samples from the area around school or home.

How to identify colour

A colour chart used internationally is the American Munsell Colour Chart. Make your own as shown in figure 1, using colour strips from paint shade cards. The British Standard number is written below each strip on the chart to make sure that you obtain the correct colour. Write to a paint manufacturer or visit a specialist paint shop to ask for a B.S. paint shade card. Explain why you wish to be so precise about the colours.

Place the Soil Colour Chart over each soil sample in turn and record the number and colour of the closest matching shade on the chart.

How to check texture

Wet a handful of soil and squeeze it until no more water comes out. Work it in your hands for about half a min-ute and then try to press it into shapes, starting with a cone and working towards a smooth bent worm.

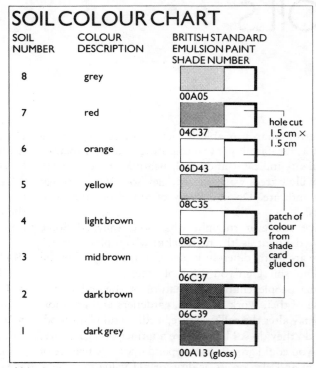

SOIL COLOUR CHART

SOIL NUMBER	COLOUR DESCRIPTION	BRITISH STANDARD EMULSION PAINT SHADE NUMBER
8	grey	00A05
7	red	04C37
6	orange	06D43
5	yellow	08C35
4	light brown	08C37
3	mid brown	06C37
2	dark brown	06C39
1	dark grey	00A13 (gloss)

hole cut 1.5 cm × 1.5 cm

patch of colour from shade card glued on

Make the chart on white card, or on white paper carefully glued onto card such as a cereal packet. Cover the chart with transparent adhesive so that it can be wiped clean after use.

Figure 1 How to make a Soil Colour Chart

SHAPE	SOIL TEXTURE
Cone	Sand
Ball	Loamy sand
Worm or roll	Loam
Bent worm which cracks	Clayey loam
Smooth bent worm	Clay

If, for example, you can make only the first two shapes then your soil is loamy sand.

How to test acidity

Unless you are sure that the soil contains very little clay, put equal quantities of barium sulphate and soil – about a thimbleful of each – into a test-tube, and then add the same quantity of distilled water. Shake the tube vigorously so that the contents mix.

If using Universal Indicator Fluid, draw off some of the liquid, perhaps with a pipette, and put this into another test-tube, then add Universal Indicator Fluid. Again shake it vigorously and compare the colour with the closest matching colour block on the pH chart. Trial and error is needed sometimes until you find the required amount of Universal Indicator Fluid. Remember this when you are in the field.

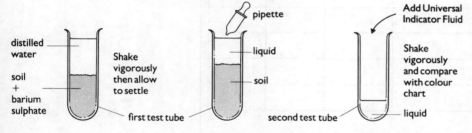

Figure 2 Testing soil acidity

If using pH papers, tilt the test-tube and quickly dip the paper into the liquid. Tap the strip against the side of the test-tube to remove excess liquid, and then compare the strip to the closest matching colour block on the pH chart.

I : To make a detailed investigation of a soil profile

PREPARATION

Make copies of the Soil Recording Sheet on page 86.

EQUIPMENT

* **Basic fieldkit** including **base-map of scale 1:25 000** (field boundaries are shown on this scale) or bigger
* **Small spade** *or* **soil auger** *or* **trowel** *or* **metal kitchen spoon**
* **1 150 mg plastic carton**
* **Polythene bags** big enough to hold 2 cartonfuls of soil, and slips of paper for identifying the samples
* **Metre rule**
* **Soil Recording Sheets**
* **Soil Colour Chart**
* **Test-tube, distilled water, barium sulphate** and *either* **Universal Indicator Fluid and colour chart** *or* **small-range (4.5 to 7.5) pH papers** *or* **mechanical pH meter**
* **Lengths of white card** or cereal packet card covered with white paper
* **Camera** (optional)

FIELDWORK METHOD

If the profile is already visible as in a river bank or artificial cutting, the 'edge' of the visible part may be weathered, so carefully remove with a trowel or metal spoon about 1 cm to reach the fresh, unweathered profile.

It is best to do as much work as possible in the field but if the weather is very wet record only the following: vegetation growing in the soil, depth of each horizon beneath the surface and position on slope. Collect two cartonfuls of material from each horizon to analyse in school or at home. Put each sample into a polythene bag labelled with the depth beneath the surface, and, if possible, the code letter and description of the horizon.

I How to recognise horizons

Horizons often blend into one another but are more clearly recognisable if you are able to stand back one

SOIL RECORDING SHEET
SITE (six-figure grid reference and additional details)

SKETCH OF
PROFILE
Label the horizons

DETAILS OF PROFILE

HORIZON	DEPTH IN CM FROM SURFACE	THICKNESS OF HORIZON	COLOUR	TEXTURE	pH VALUE

PLANTS GROWING IN THE SOIL: _____

PARENT MATERIAL (IF UNSURE LOOK AT A
GEOLOGICAL MAP): _____

LAND USE: _____

HEIGHT ABOVE SEA LEVEL: _____

ANGLE OF SLOPE: _____ DOWNHILL _____ UPHILL

ASPECT: _____

metre or more from the profile. To enable you to see them clearly when working close up to the profile, mark the boundary of each by drawing the trowel along it to make a shallow groove.

Sketch the profile in the space on your soil recording sheet.

2 Sticky tape profile

If the soil is fairly dry, place sticky tape against it so that particles from the entire depth of the profile will stick to it. Fix this onto the white card to take it home (figure 3). Check the depths of the horizons in case your sticky tape sample becomes dislodged on the way home.

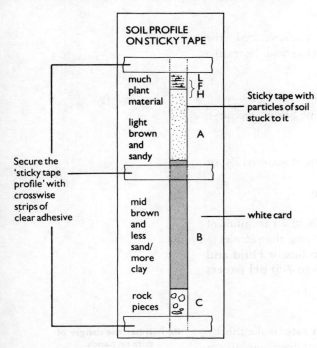

SOIL PROFILE ON STICKY TAPE

much plant material — L F H

light brown and sandy — A

Sticky tape with particles of soil stuck to it

Secure the 'sticky tape' profile with crosswise strips of clear adhesive

mid brown and less sand/ more clay — B

white card

rock pieces — C

Figure 3 An imaginary soil profile on sticky tape

Alternatively, a profile may be made at home or at school from the samples collected and the depths of horizons recorded.

Complete your 'sticky tape profile' by giving the code letter of each horizon on one side and on the other side a description of each.

3 Colour, pH and texture

Place your Soil Colour Chart against each horizon and decide which numbered colour it matches best. Record this on your Soil Recording Sheet, together with any other details such as 'contains angular fragments of rock', 'mottled', 'contains light streaks'.

Choose one method of measuring the pH value of a sample of each horizon, using either Universal Indicator Fluid or small-range pH indicator strips. If it is difficult to get a good match with the pH colour chart, describe the colour change you notice.

Take a handful of soil from each horizon and work it into different shapes as explained on page 84. Record the texture in the appropriate place on the Soil Recording Sheet.

PROCESSING THE INFORMATION

Either carefully fold up your sticky tape soil profile and include it in your finished work, or display it on a wall.

Measure the depth of the different horizons and draw a diagram on a smaller scale to put into your completed project. Label each horizon with information on colour, texture and pH.

DRAWING CONCLUSIONS

1 Describe in detail, using illustrations, the soil profile(s) which you have investigated.

2 Describe the similarities and contrasts between the topsoil and the subsoil of the profile(s) you have investigated. Suggest reasons for these.

3 Having examined the soil in detail, suggest what would be the advantages and problems it would pose for one or more of the following civil engineering projects:
(a) building a house;
(b) excavating a channel to take pipes for water, sewerage, telephone wires, cable television, electricity;
(c) building a new road;
(d) constructing a small reservoir for drinking water.

4 Test this hypothesis:
'That the parent material has little effect upon overlying soil.'

FURTHER SUGGESTIONS

I

Investigate soil profiles at different sites across a valley – a transect of ½ km is a sensible distance – to reveal either:
(a) the effects of slope, vegetation and drainage upon the development of the soil profile; or
(b) the relationship between slope and land use upon the development of the soil profile.

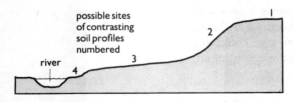

Figure 4 Section to show where variations in soil characteristics may be found

2

Use a soil profile in the centre of an area approximately ½ km × ½ km to attempt an investigation of the environmental factors affecting an ecosystem. (An ecosystem is a particular self-contained environment in which inputs and outputs 'attempt' to balance one another.) Investigate the inputs (processes which contribute to the soil) and the outputs (products which are removed from the soil).

2 : To investigate the ways in which people alter the topsoil for various purposes

FIELDWORK AREAS
Choose different sites such as a garden flower bed – the outside edge and centre; school playing field; beneath a hedge; farmland.

PREPARATION
Make a copy of the Topsoil Recording Sheet (opposite).

EQUIPMENT
- **Basic fieldkit** including base-map of scale 1:1250 or 1:2500
- **Trowel** or **metal kitchen spoon**
- **1 150 g plastic carton**
- **Polythene bags** big enough to hold 2 cartonfuls of soil, and slips of paper for identifying the samples
- **Test-tube and pH Universal Indicator Fluid and colour chart** *or* **small-range (4.5 to 7.5) pH papers** *or* **mechanical pH meter**
- **Soil Colour Chart**
- **Ruler**
- **Can to measure the infiltration rate**: make this by removing both ends of a tin can larger than 10 cm tall. Cover the rough ends thickly with sticky tape or

Remember the danger of cuts on hands.

TOPSOIL RECORDING SHEET			
LOCATION	middle of rose bed 578 718	playing field 578 717	under hawthorn hedge 575 711
DESCRIPTION OF VEGETATION			
COLOUR: At surface			
At 15 cm depth			
INFILTRATION RATE			
TEXTURE: 1 Worked in hands			
2 Sieving results			
3 Sedimentation results			
pH VALUE			
WATER CONTENT			
ORGANIC CONTENT			

sticking plaster to avoid cutting yourself.

Halfway up, inside the can, paint a coloured line, and 2 cm higher paint another line, preferably in a different colour.

Extra equipment for investigating soil texture, water content and organic content:
- **Topsoil Recording Sheet**
- **1 kitchen flour sieve** and
- **1 coffee sieve** or a **set of soil sieves**
- **Glass measuring cylinders** or **straight-sided clear-glass coffee jars**, the 150 g size is ideal. 1 for each sample collected
- **Oven**
- **Chemical balance**
- **Crucible**
- **Bunsen Burner**

FIELDWORK METHOD

At each site carry out investigations in the order given below and in exactly the same way each time. Record your results on the Topsoil Recording Sheet.

1 Location

Record the location by a six-figure grid reference, and describe any details such as 'southern edge of rose bed'; 'hawthorn hedge 1½ m high'.

2 Colour

Use your Soil Colour Chart to decide on the number and colour description of the soil. Soil at the surface may be slightly different from that at a depth of 15 cm so look out for this.

3 Testing the pH value

Use the method you preferred when preparing for your fieldwork to measure the pH of the soil. As with colour, there may be a difference in pH value between 'surface soil' and that further down. Test and see.

4 Infiltration rate

Infiltration is the term used to describe the way in which rainfall enters the soil. The infiltration rate, sometimes called the **infiltration capacity**, depends upon many factors, including the soil's texture and the amount of water already in the soil. The infiltration rate in a ploughed field is almost double that of heavily grazed pasture land.

You should carry out the investigations within an hour or two at each of your chosen soil sites, so it is likely that they will have received the same amount of rainfall in the time prior to your fieldwork. Find out from a local weather station what the rainfall has been during the previous week.

To measure the infiltration rate half bury the can in the soil, so that the lower painted ring is level with the surface of the soil. Fill the 2 cm between the two rings with water and record in seconds the length of time for the water level to drop from the upper ring to the lower one. Express this in centimetres per second: for example

$$\frac{2 \text{ cm}}{10 \text{ sec}} = 0.2 \text{ cm/sec}$$

5 Collecting samples

Dig to a depth of 15 cm and collect two cartonfuls of soil. If you have discovered differences in colour and pH value between the surface soil and that deeper down, then put a cartonful of 'surface' soil and one of deeper soil each into a separate polythene bag. Label the samples as precisely as possible.

The next three tests are to be carried out in school or at home.

6 Investigating texture

There are three different ways of identifying soil texture.

(i)   By working the soil into different shapes as described on page 84.

(ii) By sedimentation. Put one cartonful of soil into a coffee jar or measuring cylinder and add two cartonfuls of water. Label the sample and shake with a lid on or stir vigorously. Leave the soil to settle for 24 hours.

Clay particles may remain suspended for a very long time – sometimes weeks. By the end of the investigation the water above the soil should be clear; if it is not clear within a few hours you may decide to add barium sulphate to help the clay particles to combine in clumps and sink more rapidly to the bottom. Measure the depth of the various layers using a ruler or the graduations on the side of the measuring cylinder ($1 \text{ cm}^3 = 1 \text{ ml}$).

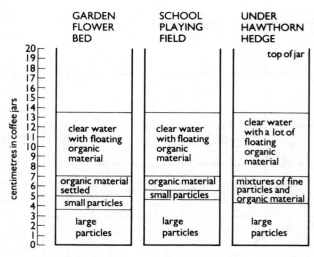

Figure 5 Comparing soil textures by sedimentation

Record your results by making a drawing of your container and sample. The results of one such investigation are shown in figure 5.

(iii) By sieving. The soil must be dried so this investigation may easily be done after the test for water content. Use either kitchen sieves, as in figure 6, or a set of soil sieves. Soil sieves are so accurate that the soil sample will be divided into six different classes of particle size.

FLOUR SIEVE
Metal sieves hold particles of 2 mm diameter and larger. Plastic sieves hold particles of 1 mm diameter and larger
= LARGE PARTICLES

COFFEE SIEVE
holds particles of 0.5 mm and more
= MEDIUM PARTICLES

PAPER collects particles of diameter smaller than 0.5 mm
= SMALL PARTICLES

Figure 6 Sieving soil

The official size of different particles is measured as the diameter in millimetres. The following are the major classes:

sand   0.2–2.0
silt   0.002–0.2
clay   less than 0.002

Next, measure the volume of soil of each particle size by putting each in turn into a measuring cylinder like the one used for a rain gauge (see page 70). You can make your own from a cardboard tube by glueing a graduated strip of paper inside it. Calculate the volume of each particle size as a percentage of the whole sample. Classify the soil

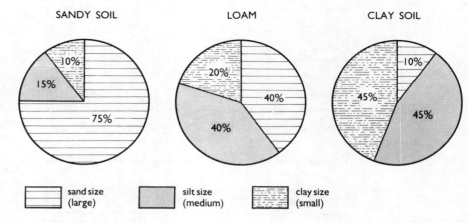

SANDY SOIL   LOAM   CLAY SOIL

10% 15% 75%

20% 40% 40%

10% 45% 45%

sand size (large)   silt size (medium)   clay size (small)

Figure 7 Pie-charts to compare soil textures

according to the pie-chart in figure 7 which most closely resembles it.

7 Testing water content

Use a chemical balance to weigh an equal volume of each of your soil samples saturated with water. Put the sample into a container and add water slowly until a layer of water begins to lie on top. The soil is then saturated. Record the weight of each.

Put each sample into an oven at about 90°C – cool enough not to destroy the organic material in the soil. Leave them for 2 to 3 hours to dry out completely and then weigh each again. Subtract the second weight from the first to calculate the water loss. 1 gram of water = 1 cm^3.

Copy and complete the table on page 92.

Compare the results in the table. You may be able to suggest whether the soil, when you investigated the infiltration rate, was near to its maximum water content, sometimes called **field capacity**. Was it closer to complete dryness?

SOIL TYPE	WATER CONTENT	INFILTRATION RATE

8 Testing the organic material content

Plant remains burn out if the soil is heated to a temperature of about 500–600°C. Weigh two 5 ml spoonfuls of dry soil on a chemical balance and then put them into a crucible. Place the crucible containing the soil on a tripod over a Bunsen burner and heat it gently at first to avoid cracking the porcelain crucible. When the crucible becomes hot, increase the flame – open the air hole – and heat very strongly. The organic material turns into a gas, often visible, as it burns. When the gas disappears let the crucible cool and then weigh the soil again. To make sure that your results are as accurate as possible, repeat the heating and re-weighing until a constant weight is obtained. Calculate the weight of the organic material as a percentage of the soil:

$$\frac{\text{weight of organic material}}{\text{weight of unburnt soil}} \times 100$$

Calcium carbonate and a small part of the clay particles may also have been burnt so that the organic material content of a clay soil may be over-estimated.

In your results, compare the organic content of the different soils. Give your opinion of the extent to which organic materials have been added to the soil to provide plant nutrients. Organic material is an important source of plant food when dissolved in the soil water.

DRAWING CONCLUSIONS

1 Describe the similarities and contrasts between soils investigated from different localities, such as:
   (a) playing field/lawn and flower bed;
   (b) pasture and land under crops;
   (c) pasture and playing field.
   Suggest reasons for your comparisons.

2 Imagine that you are:
   (a) a gardener trying to grow a large variety of plants on a small area. Describe the advantages of the soil in your area and explain what has to be done to improve and maintain fertility (texture and nutrient value);
   (b) a farmer who must maintain the fertility of your land. Explain the ways in which crop rotations are important and the reasons for cultivating and fertilizing the soil;
   (c) a groundsman who must maintain hockey/football pitches, or bring a cricket pitch or golf course up to competition standard. Describe the ways in which you would tackle the work season by season.

3 Test this hypothesis: 'That soils may be altered for various purposes.'

FURTHER SUGGESTIONS

I

An adult sheep may weigh anything from 90 to 135 kg, according to its breed. Each foot exerts a pressure of 2.75–5.0 kg per cm^2.

Pressure may be calculated as a ratio between the

total body weight and the area of land with which it is in direct contact. Find out the pressures exerted by the feet of other grazing animals and by farm machinery or that used in a garden or on a playing field. Assess the effects of each upon different soil textures and drainage conditions.

2

Collect two or more contrasting types of soil, noting the location where each was obtained. Place these in wooden trays or egg cartons. Grow from seed such plants as marigold or antirrhinum in each soil sample and observe differences in growth. Compare results and suggest ways in which you could alter the soil to improve the growth.

3

Plot on a map areas of derelict land. Investigate the topsoil on one or more of these areas, and then suggest ways in which the soil could be improved to allow the land to be reclaimed for public use.

STREAMS

How does a stream make a channel for itself? Suggest ways in which erosion, transport of the load and deposition alter the shape of the channel.

A stream transports a load of alluvium. This is material from the valley sides which has moved downwards into the stream, and material which the stream itself erodes from the bed and banks of the channel in which it flows. It transports the load by any of three main methods (figure 1).

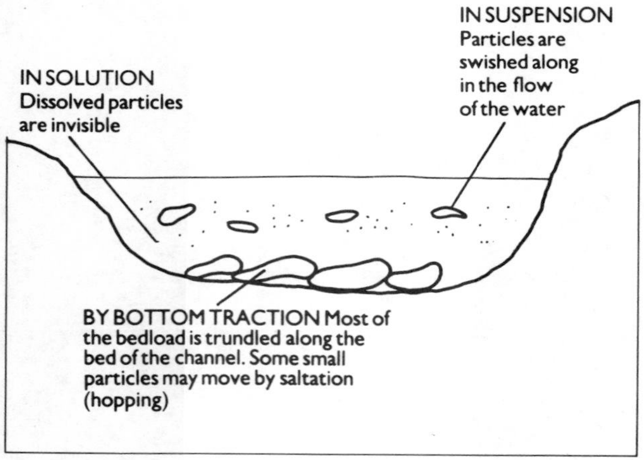

According to the number of tributaries a stream has received it may be classed into a hierarchy called **stream order**. This enables comparison of different streams to be made irrespective of their size. Can you work out from figure 2 the system for classifying streams?

When choosing your stream, make sure that it has public access or, if necessary, obtain permission from the owner. This may not be possible where the stream is used for fishing or drinking water.

SAFETY is vital in choosing the location of your stream investigation. Never wade into a stream deeper than 5 cm below your knee. Remember that if you slip and bang your head on a rock you could drown yourself in water only 10 cm deep.

IN SOLUTION
Dissolved particles
are invisible

IN SUSPENSION
Particles are
swished along
in the flow
of the water

BY BOTTOM TRACTION Most of
the bedload is trundled along the
bed of the channel. Some small
particles may move by saltation
(hopping)

Figure 1 Diagram to show how a stream transports its load

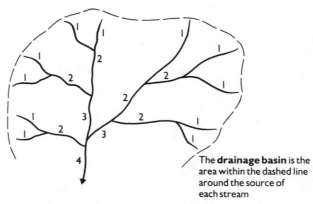

The **drainage basin** is the area within the dashed line around the source of each stream

Figure 2 Diagram to show how streams within a drainage basin may be classified into orders

When the channel is full of water the stream is said to be in its **bankfull** stage. If the water level rises above bankfull it is in **flood**.

FIELDWORK AREAS

A small stream of any order is very similar to a much bigger stream of the same order. From a small scale

Ordnance Survey map such as the 1:250 000, trace a river system in which all the streams eventually drain into the main one. Mark the edge of the **drainage basin** with a dashed line as in figure 2. Next, number each stream according to its order. Decide upon one or more locations for your fieldwork. Note each with a six-figure grid reference.

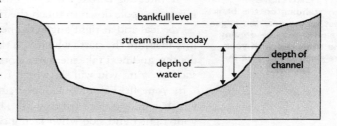

Figure 3 Section through an imaginary stream to show bankfull level

1 : To measure the cross-section of the channel and the depth of water it contains

PREPARATION

Copy the Table for Recording Stream and Channel Measurements into your field notebook. Figure 3 shows the measurements that you will make.

Make a list of problems you may come across and try to work out ways of solving them.

EQUIPMENT
- **Basic fieldkit** including base-map of scale 1:1250 or 1:2500
- **Tape measure** with centimetre markings
- **Plumb lines:** Tie a heavy metal weight, at least 1 kg, securely on the end of a piece of cord such as a washing line: part of an old metal pipe would be ideal. Tie pieces of bias binding of different colours into the cord at intervals of 10 cm from the weight.
  and/or
- **Graduated poles:** Paint poles made of, e.g., dowelling, in stripes of two distinctive colours at 10 cm intervals.
- **Length of cord to span the stream**
- **Table for Recording Stream and Channel Measurements**
- **Spirit level**
- **Heavy stones to act as weights** *or*
- **tent pegs**

FIELDWORK METHOD
Stretch a piece of cord or pole from one bank to the other. It should be ½ m wider than the channel on both sides. Secure it at each end with a heavy stone or tent peg and pull it taut. Use the spirit level to make sure it is horizontal.

TABLE FOR RECORDING STREAM AND CHANNEL MEASUREMENTS

DATE	WIDTH OF BANKFULL SURFACE	WIDTH OF STREAM TODAY	DEPTH OF CHANNEL AT INTERVALS ACROSS BANKFULL LEVEL	DEPTH OF WATER AT INTERVALS ACROSS CHANNEL TODAY

CAUTION:
When standing on the bank do not go too near the edge. The river may be eroding the bank and with your weight it could cave in.

At intervals across the cord dip the plumb line or measuring pole down to touch the river bed. Each must be vertical and at right angles to the cord or pole. If you first measure the parts which you think are of different depths, and next take measurements at regular intervals such as ½ m, you will see which is the better method.

In your field notebook make sure that you record which bank you are starting at. The right bank is on your right hand side when facing downstream.

Repeat the method in exactly the same way at every location you intend to investigate.

PROCESSING THE INFORMATION

1 Drawing a section/profile to scale
The horizontal and vertical scales must be the same. Draw your section on graph paper, using the biggest scale possible. Draw the surface of the water to represent the depth on the date of your fieldwork. Draw the bankfull surface as a dashed line.

NOTE
This method can also be used for the measurement of area on a map.

2 Calculating the cross-sectional area of the channel
Count the number of complete squares covered by water, and include those where half or more than half of a square is covered. Do not count squares which are less than half covered.

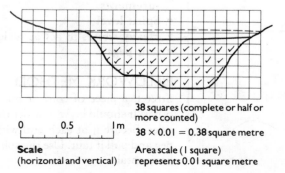

38 squares (complete or half or more counted)

38 × 0.01 = 0.38 square metre

Scale
(horizontal and vertical)

0   0.5   1 m

Area scale (1 square)
represents 0.01 square metre

Figure 4 How to measure area

Multiply the number of squares by your scale and the result is the area in square metres. This measurement is the area of the channel holding water. Calculate what percentage this is of the area at the bankfull level.

DRAWING CONCLUSIONS
1 Describe what your investigations and calculations show about the shape of the river's channel and the depth of water it contains.
2 Test one of these hypotheses:
   (a) 'That the water in the channel on (date of fieldwork) was only a small percentage of the bankfull capacity.'
   (b) 'That the shape of the channel alters with the order of the stream that has made it.'

FURTHER SUGGESTIONS

1
Using the same method, repeat your investigations on a different part of the stream. A straight stretch and a meander may provide an interesting contrast. Compare the width of the channel with its maximum depth at each location. Does the ratio vary or is it fairly constant? Suggest reasons for your conclusion.

2
Investigate a stream of higher or lower order and compare and contrast your findings.

3
Return to the same location at other times. Try to explain any changes in terms of recent rainfall. Figures can be obtained by writing to your local Water Authority or to the nearest meteorological station. The addresses may be found in the public library or in the telephone directory. Look at geological maps to see if

any of the rainfall may be stored in the rocks. What is the land use in the fields near the stream?

4

Do you think the channel you studied has been altered by people? Can you see evidence of mills, weirs, locks or towpaths, for example?

2 : To investigate the speed of flow of the stream's surface

PREPARATION

What slows down the speed of flow of a stream apart from friction with the air? Where do you think the water's speed of flow in each of the three cross-sections in figure 5 is fastest?

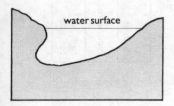 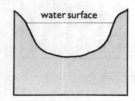 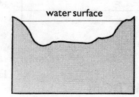

Figure 5 The cross-section of three possible stream channels

The fieldwork will have to be done in pairs or groups and you must be able to see each other easily. Draw a large-scale map of the part of the stream you intend to investigate. The scale must be at least 1:2500.

Obtain 30 floats which will give reliable results, such as dog biscuits of the same shape and size, or the peel of a quartered orange. What else could you use that would

Be sure that you can see one another, both for safety and to make the work easier

not pollute the river or countryside? Mark 10 floats with one bright colour and another 10 with a different colour; the remainder may be left plain. Why is it more accurate to time the floats 10 times and calculate the average? Why might one time only be misleading?

EQUIPMENT
- **Basic fieldkit including map of scale 1:1250 or 1:2500**
- **30 floats**
- **Stopwatch**
- **Cord(s)**
- **Table for Recording Speed of Flow (page 98)**

FIELDWORK METHOD

Three floats must be dropped simultaneously into the stream, one at each side and one in the middle of the stream. If only one person is available to do this then spear three yoghurt cartons on a rod and put one float in each. The floats can then be tipped out simultaneously. This will need practice! Each float must be a different colour.

The Starter should weight one end of the cord with a stone and throw it across to the Timer on the opposite bank. Both should draw the cord taut and fasten it at both ends with a heavy stone or tent peg, or to the root of a tree. Pace out 50 m, or other suitable distance, downstream and, if possible, stretch another cord across the stream to mark the finishing line.

Together decide which colour of float you will use to time the flow of water on the right bankside (your right-hand side as you look downstream), midstream and left bankside. Decide upon the signals which the Starters will use as they drop the floats simultaneously into the water: waving an arm or blowing a whistle. The Timer must let the Starters know when to drop the next set of floats into the water.

The Timer begins the timing immediately he/she receives the signal and records the time taken for each float to reach him. The results should be recorded in a table like this:

TABLE FOR RECORDING SPEED OF FLOW		
LEFT-BANK FLOAT (blue paint)	MIDSTREAM FLOAT (red paint)	RIGHT-BANK FLOAT (no paint)

PROCESSING THE INFORMATION

1 Calculating the speed of flow

Calculate the average speed of each set of ten floats. Divide the distance covered by the average time taken and express this in distance per second.

$$\text{average speed} = \frac{\text{distance}}{\text{average time}}$$

The top layers of water in a stream move faster than the bottom layers. If you multiply your value for the average speed (which is the speed of the top layer) by 0.8, you will get an average value for the speed of the whole stream. 0.8 is a value reached by geographers after many years of investigation of the flow of the water surface.

2 Bar-chart

Draw a bar-chart to show either the average distance covered per second by each float or the average speed of each float over the 'paced' distance. If you draw this beside your sketch-map it could help you to explain differences in the speed of the water.

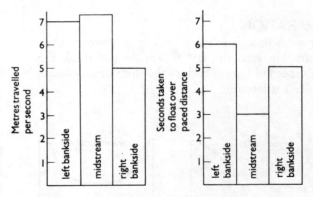

Figure 6 Bar-charts to show the speed of flow of the stream

3 Sketch-map

In order to show the course taken by each float in the water you will need to enlarge your base map to a scale of at least 1:500. Does this help to explain the different speeds of the floats?

DRAWING CONCLUSIONS

1 Describe, with illustrations, what your investigations and calculations show about the speed of flow of the surface of the stream.

2 Describe the effect of the shape of the channel cross-

section on the speed of flow of the surface water in different parts of the channel.

3 Test one of these hypotheses:

(a) 'That the water in midstream flows quicker than that nearest to the bank.'

(b) 'That the water flows quickest on the outer side of a meander.'

FURTHER SUGGESTIONS

1

Return to the area after a period of heavier or lighter rainfall, and repeat your investigations in exactly the same way. Describe the contrasts and similarities you discover.

2

If you have a flow meter, measure the speed of the water at different depths below the surface.

3

Flood prevention schemes often alter the shape of a river's channel to make it more efficient in draining the area. Imagine that you are a planner in the Water Authority of your drainage basin. Describe, with reasons, the ways in which you would make the stream's channel more efficient so as to remove water more quickly. Remember that you would have to gain permission to use private land, and not cause damage to farming, housing or leisure areas.

3 : To investigate stream discharge

PREPARATION

The stream's discharge is the amount of water passing a point on the channel. It is measured in **cumecs**, which means the number of cubic metres of water passing through the channel at one particular place in one second. Measuring the discharge is important to people responsible for water supply, flood control and the provision of water sports.

Discharge is related to weather, geology and land use in the drainage basin, so obtain information on each of these from a meteorological station within the drainage basin, and from maps of the solid geology and drift geology and land use within the drainage basin.

EQUIPMENT

- **Basic fieldkit including base-map of scale 1:10 000**
- **Equipment** used for Investigations 1 and 2 (pages 95 and 97)

FIELDWORK METHOD

At your chosen location(s) measure and record in your field notebook the cross-sectional area of water as explained on pages 95–6 and the speed of flow of the water as explained on pages 97–8.

PROCESSING THE INFORMATION

1 Calculation

Follow the instructions in the corresponding sections of Investigations 1 and 2. Multiply the speed of flow (distance per second) by the cross-sectional area (calculated in square metres), and the result will be the discharge. If the stream is very small it would be sensible to express the discharge in litres per second. Do this by multiplying the number of cumecs by 1000. There are 1000 litres in 1 cubic metre.

2 Sketch-map and flow-line map

On your sketch-map use a flow-line map drawn to scale to

show the discharge at every location where you measured it. The width of the flow arrow must represent the number of cumecs of water (figure 7). Add this scale to your map.

3 Bar-chart for results at different locations
If you have measured the discharge at different locations, draw bar-charts and place them from left to right in rank order. Identify each location with a six-figure grid reference, and give the order of the stream.

DRAWING CONCLUSIONS
1 Describe what your investigations and calculations show about stream discharge.
2 Describe the similarities and differences between the discharge at different locations and suggest reasons for them from your observations.

Figure 7 Flow-line map to show stream discharge

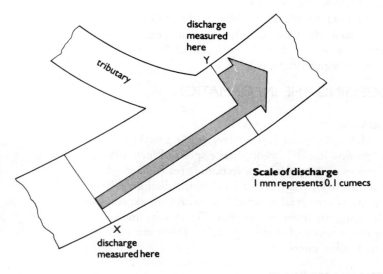

3 Test one or more of these hypotheses:
  (a) 'That the discharge remains almost constant until the stream receives a tributary.'
  (b) 'That the discharge is much greater on streams of higher order within the same drainage basin.'
  (c) 'That the discharge is affected very little by differences in the shape of the cross-section of the channel.'

FURTHER SUGGESTIONS

1
(a) It is interesting to discover just how much water you and your family use each day:
    50 litres for flushing the WC
    45 litres to wash yourself and have a bath or shower
    14 litres for washing up
    14 litres for washing clothes and cleaning the home
     5 litres for food and drink
    Make observations and try to calculate the amount you use. Why not compare figures for a weekday with a day at the weekend? What differences do you find, if any?
(b) An average of 2.5 people live in each home in this country. Calculate the discharge in 24 hours of the stream you have investigated. How many households could your stream supply with water?
(c) Choose one grid square on a 1:10 000 scale Ordnance Survey map and count the number of buildings. Calculate their average water needs and discover where the water supply comes from.

2
Return to your fieldwork location to repeat your investigations at different times of the year. Obtain the rainfall figures for the same time. Either plot both discharge and rainfall on a scattergraph, or draw a bar-chart of

rainfall and mark the discharge above the appropriate month.

3
Look at the solid geology map and the land use map of the catchment area of the stream(s) you have investigated. Estimate the percentage of the area under limestone and chalk, forest and buildings. These will all slow down the rate of discharge. Do you think they may have affected your results?

4 : To investigate material transported by the stream

PREPARATION

How does a stream get energy? Write down the ways in which a stream's energy could be increased or decreased.

Look again at figure 1 on page 94, which shows the different ways a stream transports its load. The recognised sizes of the length (long axis) of some particles are given on page 106. When would you expect to find pebbles in the suspension load? When would you expect to find a lot of sand in the bed load?

The solution load is extremely difficult to investigate, needing the sort of equipment you use in chemistry lessons. Investigation of the suspension load is difficult unless the stream is carrying a lot of material in this way. However, fieldwork on the river bed material alone can be interesting and informative.

You may choose to investigate different parts of one stream, or similar parts of several streams. Draw a map of scale 1:50 000 to show the location of the places you intend to investigate.

EQUIPMENT

- **Basic fieldkit** including base-map of scale 1:1250 or 1:2500

- **Scoop securely fastened to the end of a pole**: the scoop could be a plastic dustpan, or bucket
- **1 kitchen flour sieve**
- **1 tea or coffee sieve**
- **Ruler**
- **Measuring tape**
- **Watertight containers for specimens**: Large polythene boxes or tubs with a lid
- **Cord**
- **Spring-balance and polythene bag**

EXTRA EQUIPMENT FOR INVESTIGATION OF MATERIAL CARRIED IN SUSPENSION:
- **Yoghurt carton** attached either to a cord or to a pole: a weight attached to the cord will enable you to take samples beneath the surface
- **Watertight containers** such as large polythene cartons

FIELDWORK METHOD

1 Investigation of material on the stream bed
If there is little water in the stream you may see big boulders brought down at some time when the stream was in flood. Measure the biggest particle: it may be a huge piece of rock.

Weight the end of the cord and throw it across the stream to your friend on the opposite bank. Pull the cord tight and secure it at each end with a stone or around a tree root. The line it makes will be the baseline to enable you to take a systematic random sample of the load.

At regular intervals, such as ½ metre, across the line of the cord fill the scoop as full as possible with material. Measure systematically from the right bankside to the left bankside. This will be a systematic random sample. Put samples into separate containers clearly labelled

Do not go too near the edge of the bank.

on the lid: '½ m from right bankside'; '1 m from right bankside', and so on.

2 Investigation of the suspension load

Collect samples close to both banks and one in mid-stream. Lower the yoghurt carton below the surface but avoid touching the bed. Fill two cartons each time and place the contents of both into one watertight container. Label each sample clearly on the lid; 'right bankside', 'midstream' or 'left bankside'.

Take all samples collected home or back to school ready for measuring.

3 Measuring samples of inorganic stream material

Draw tables similar to the one below for

1. material collected from the bed of the stream;
2. material collected from the suspension load.

Allow the samples to dry out completely. To speed this up, empty them into separate, clean tins and put them in an oven set at a low temperature for half an hour. Take care to keep the samples separate.

Pour each sample when cold into a polythene bag and weigh it as accurately as possible. Use the same weighing equipment, scales or spring-balance, for each. Record the weight of each sample in the top column of the table.

Work systematically through the samples as follows:

1. Put the particles into the flour sieve and shake it. Those particles which remain in the sieve have a diameter of more than 1.5 mm and are coarse material. Weigh these particles and record them on the table.
2. Put the particles which have passed through the flour sieve into the coffee sieve. Riddle this to separate the particles of intermediate size (0.5 mm – 1.5 mm) from the finest ones. Weigh each category and record the result on the table. (See figure 6, page 91.)

PROCESSING THE INFORMATION

1 Sketch-map

A sketch-map of scale 1:50 000 will probably be big enough for you to locate with an arrow the place of investigation. Add the date on which you carried out the fieldwork and the six-figure grid reference.

2 Displaying samples

Put samples into polythene bags and include them in the account of your investigation, perhaps around your sketch-map. Label each with the six-figure grid reference of the location where you collected them, and indicate from which part of the stream's cross-section you obtained each.

Most of your samples will consist of particles of rock,

SYSTEMATIC RANDOM SAMPLES TAKEN AT GRID REFERENCE					
	LEFT BANKSIDE	3 m INTERVALS	2 m ACROSS	I m STREAM	RIGHT BANKSIDE
DRY WEIGHT OF TOTAL SAMPLE					
WEIGHT OF COARSE MATERIAL					
WEIGHT OF INTERMEDIATE SIZE OF MATERIAL					
WEIGHT OF FINE MATERIAL					

sand and other inorganic material. There may be twigs, leaves or other vegetation and evidence of pollution such as paper, matches, bottle tops. Remove these from each sample and make a note of the contents.

3 Bar-charts to show the variations in the material sampled

For each group of results (stream bed material and suspension load at each location), calculate the proportion of the total weight made up by coarse material, intermediate material and fine material.

Draw a bar-chart to illustrate your findings, showing the weights of fine, intermediate and coarse material on the vertical axis and the location on the horizontal axis (figure 8).

DRAWING CONCLUSIONS

1 Describe the difference between material at the bank-sides and the midstream in (a) the stream bed material and (b) the suspension load. Refer to your results and suggest reasons from your observations.
2 Describe differences in (a) the stream bed material and (b) the suspension load at the locations you have investigated. Suggest reasons from your observations in the field.
3 Does the load become of smaller average particle size downstream? Use your results to support this.
4 Test one of these hypotheses:
  (a) 'That a high-order stream contains a larger weight of suspension load than a first-order stream does.'
  (b) 'That the load becomes smaller in average particle-size as the stream becomes of higher order.'

FURTHER SUGGESTIONS

1

Has the stream's load been affected by people? Streams are used for recreation, fishing, water supply, disposal of effluent and navigation. While you were investigating the material in the stream did you notice: the presence of fish, and other creatures such as the stonefly nymph or the mayfly nymph, freshwater shrimp, or the water louse and sludge worm? These animals are indicators of the degree of water pollution. Were there cans, papers and other litter left by people?

2

What will happen to the load as the river level rises or as the river level falls? If possible, return to repeat your investigations at different river levels.

Figure 8 Cumulative bar-charts to show different stream bed materials

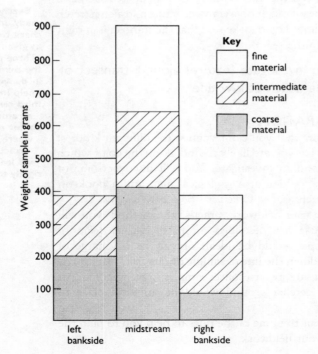

Key
fine material
intermediate material
coarse material

COASTS

Most people enjoy the seaside and through the centuries most stretches of coastline in Britain have been altered in some way. There would be no sand at Blackpool south of the Central Pier if the promenade, 11 kilometres long, had not been built about 100 years ago. The flood barrier on the River Thames at London, completed in 1984, is the biggest of its kind in the world.

Make two lists: one of reasons why people live at the seaside, and the other giving reasons why people from inland visit the seaside. Your lists will include an enormous variety, from shipyards to lighthouses, bird sanctuaries to beach huts. During your fieldwork be aware of the effect people have had on the coast.

The coast is where the sea meets the land. Have you ever thought why some coasts are rocky and some have sandy beaches or pebble beaches?

A **beach** is an assortment of loose rock fragments of different sizes accumulated on top of solid rock. Where does beach material come from and how does it get there? Write down your suggestions.

Waves are generated by the wind. In deep water only the wave, and not the water, moves forward. You can test this by sending a wave along a rope or by watching a brightly painted cork dropped from a pier into deep water.

Waves affect the coast in four different ways:
1. construction or building-up of a beach: these waves break every 9 or 10 seconds (6 or 7 per minute);
2. destruction or combing-down of a beach: when the waves break more frequently, perhaps 12 to 14 per minute;
3. lateral movement of beach material along the coast;
4. alteration of cliffs.

FIELDWORK AREAS

Most of your fieldwork will be in a small area such as a bay or headland or on a transect across a straight stretch of coastline. Try to make sure that the transect is at right angles to the sea.

1 : To investigate features along a transect of the beach at low tide

PREPARATION

Make sure that you can recognise the different kinds of rock which you are likely to find along the coast which you intend to investigate. You will discover some of these by looking at a geological map and a book on rocks, such as *The Observer's Book of Geology*.

Before your fieldwork, practise the methods you will use. These are described on page 106. A team of five people would be ideal: one to be in charge of putting down the line of sample or quadrat, two for the tape measure, two to collect samples to bring home. An area of derelict ground would be an ideal place to practise.

Find out the time of the tides to help you to plan the day of your fieldwork.

MAN-MADE FEATURES   **PHYSICAL FEATURES**

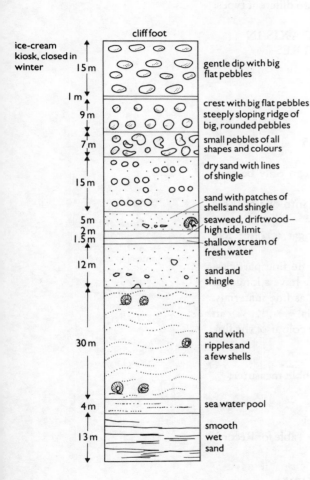

Figure 1 *Imaginary transect to show beach materials*

Scale = 1 mm represents 1 m

In your fieldwork notebook rule parallel lines to represent the length of your transect. When complete it will look something like figure 1.

Copy the Table for Recording Beach Material on page 107.

EQUIPMENT

- **Basic fieldkit** including base-map of scale 1:1250 or 1:2500
- **Cord about 10 m long**
- **Wooden rod ½ metre long**
- **Quadrat**: make one as shown in figure 2 – a square frame, 15 cm × 15 cm or larger, made from dowelling nailed at each corner
- **Plastic buckets or containers** such as old biscuit tins for collecting samples; each must be labelled carefully so put paper into each
- **Sieve** – laboratory soil sieves may be used, but a kitchen flour sieve holds particles of diameter larger than 1.5 mm and is useful for dividing beach material into 'coarse' and 'fine'
- **Pebble measurer**: glue a square of centimetre graph paper 30 cm × 30 cm onto 4 mm thick plywood or onto very strong card. Cover it with transparent adhesive so that it can be wiped clean. A set square will ensure accuracy (figure 3)
- **Weighing scale**: a spring-balance for use in the field can be bought quite cheaply at a fishing-tackle shop. A net bag used for holding vegetables is ideal for holding pebbles and attaching to the spring balance (figure 4). Kitchen scales at home could be used.
- **Table for Recording Beach Material**

FIELDWORK METHOD

Three times during your fieldwork, count the number of breakers arriving on the beach per minute. Calculate the average and record this in your field notebook.

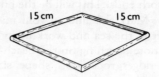

Figure 2 *Quadrat made from dowelling*

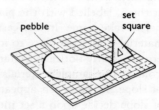

Figure 3 *How to make a pebble measurer*

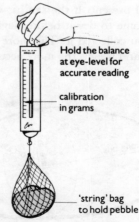

Figure 4 *How to weigh pebbles*

Lay the cord up the beach from sea level and weight it at both ends. This will be the line of transect you will follow. Mark this line on your map: → • → • → •

Start at the sea and work inland. In your field notebook note anything on the beach which interests you: beach ridges; rock pools; shape, size and colour of pebbles. To locate the feature along the transect use the tape to measure the distance from the sea.

If possible, measure the size of beach material during your fieldwork. If the weather is very bad, collect samples and put them, labelled with the place collected, into a container to take home. In any case, you could collect some material from each place to make a display.

If there are clearly noticeable changes in slope on the beach collect your sample materials from each different angle of slope. If the beach appears to be uniform in angle of slope decide upon a set interval such as every metre, or two metres, along the transect at which to collect material. At each location put down the wooden rod or quadrat across the line of the transect. Measure and/or collect the three largest particles and a handful of sand if present. If the sand is wet you will have to take it home to dry it before sieving. Label accurately where you collected it. The more samples you collect, measure and weigh, the more accurate your results will be.

All particles have three dimensions, and the length of each is called an axis (figure 5). The length of the longest axis is used to classify beach material into different types:

BEACH MATERIAL	LONGEST AXIS IN MILLIMETRES
boulders	over 200
cobbles	60–200
pebbles	5–59
shingle	2–4
sand	0.5–1.9
fine sand	less than 0.5

Silt and clay are so small that they can only be seen under a microscope.

Each particle may also be classified into one of these shapes:
(a) sphere – like a ball, (b) rod – like a cigar, (c) disc – like a coin.

As you collect each sample, sieve the fine particles. The ones which pass through the sieve have a long axis shorter than 1.5 mm and are classed as fine materials. Estimate the proportion of this material – ¾, ½, ¼ – in your sample area. Record this and the colour of the fine material.

For each of the larger particles:
1. measure the long axis with the pebble measurer;
2. weigh it;
3. record its shape;
4. describe the appearance of the rock.

Record all of this information on the Table for Recording Beach Material.

PROCESSING THE INFORMATION

I Map of the transect investigated
Draw a map of the beach. Choose a scale which will

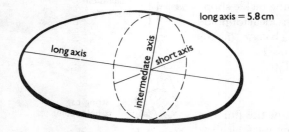

Figure 5 The dimensions of a pebble

enable you to show the reasons why you chose that particular transect and the results of your investigation. Annotate the map as in figure 1 on page 105 and add extra notes to describe cliffs, dunes, rock pools and other features of interest.

2 Model of the transect

Use white card or card from cereal packets covered with white paper and the samples you collected to make a model of the beach transect. Cut the card into a strip between 6 and 10 cm wide, with its length to scale: perhaps 1 cm to represent 1 m. Glue samples onto the card in the locations where you collected them on the beach. Label the model in detail and add the scale.

3 Assessing the relationship between pebble weight, length and shape

Draw a scattergraph as illustrated in figure 6 (overleaf), and plot the results obtained for each pebble recorded.

Draw a line around any major groupings which you find. Suggest reasons for the groupings by relating them to the rock type.

4 Description of wave type

From your timing of the breakers suggest whether on the day of your fieldwork they were beach-building or beach-destructive.

DRAWING CONCLUSIONS

1 Using your map, model and scattergraphs as illustrations, describe the distribution of materials and features on the beach transect you have investigated.
2 Give evidence of the use of the beach by people and the ways in which the beach has been altered. Suggest reasons for the alterations.
3 Test this hypothesis:
'That the shape and weight of pebbles is related to their rock type.'

FURTHER SUGGESTIONS

1

Repeat the fieldwork in a different part of the same beach or on another beach. Suggest reasons for similarities and contrasts you may find.

TABLE FOR RECORDING BEACH MATERIAL

LOCATION, INCLUDING DISTANCE FROM THE SEA	LONG AXIS IN mm	WEIGHT IN GRAMS	SHAPE	DESCRIPTION: COLOUR AND APPEARANCE OF ROCK	ROCK TYPE
Base of ridge 82·5m from sea A	31	52	disc	dark grey, flaky	shale
Base of ridge 82·5m from sea A	172	64	rod	black speckled with grey	definitely igneous probably dolerite
Base of ridge 82·5m from sea A	53	28	sphere	white pitted with little holes	chalk
Slope of ridge 89·5m from sea B	7.9	807	sphere	grey and white speckled	granite

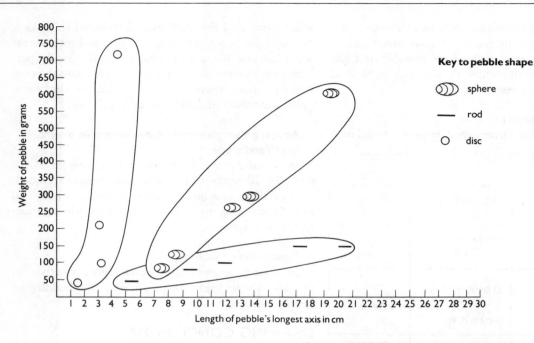

Figure 6 Scattergraph to show the size, shape and weight of pebbles

Key to pebble shape

sphere

rod

disc

2

Discover changes to the beach through history from sources such as old maps, records and postcards. People who have lived in the area for a long time are often very helpful. Try to discover reasons for the changes.

2 : To level the profile of the beach at low tide and to record the location of different types of beach material

PREPARATION

You may have sophisticated equipment for levelling, such as an alidade, Abney level and tripod, and sieves bought from laboratory suppliers for measurement of the sizes of beach material. If not, make sure that you have each piece of equipment listed, some of which you will be able to make in school or at home.

Levelling is best done with six people working as a team:

Method using a horizontal level: 1 leveller to do the sighting, 1 to make sure that the level is horizontal, 1 to hold the measuring staff, 2 to use the tape measure, 1 to record results.

Method using a bucket of water and plastic tube: 1 to hold the plastic tube, 1 to assist in keeping the plastic tube still and the bucket filled with water, 1 to hold the measuring staff, 2 to use the tape measure, 1 to record results.

Method using a clinometer: 1 to sight through the clinometer, 1 to read the angle of slope, 1 to hold the measuring staff, 2 to use the tape measure, 1 to record results.

The beach material measuring team will be made up of five people: 1 to place the metre rule or piece of timber in position, 1 to collect sample material, 1 to measure the size of sample particles, 1 to weigh the samples, 1 to record the location.

It is sensible to practise before your fieldwork the method you will use for levelling and for measuring beach material.

Make a copy of the Levelling Recording Sheet for the method you are going to use (page 110 or page 112).

EQUIPMENT
- **Basic fieldkit, including base-map of scale 1:1250 or 1:2500**

LEVELLING EQUIPMENT
- **Cord** long enough to cover the whole or a large part of the beach transect chosen
- **Measuring staff** made from a pole 2 m high with each ¼ m painted alternately in red and white and marked off in centimetres in black
- **Tape measure**
- **Graph paper**
- **Levelling Recording Sheet**
- **Horizontal level** – this can be made easily and cheaply as illustrated in figure 7

  or
- **An alidade** – this needs a stand such as tripod or projector stand. It is essential that the alidade be horizontal for sighting

  or
- **Bucket and tube**: a plastic bucket and approximately 10 m of transparent plastic tubing

  or

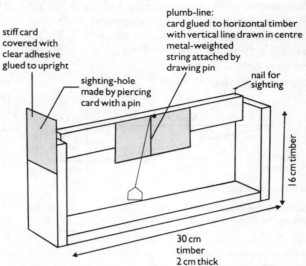

Figure 7 How to make a level

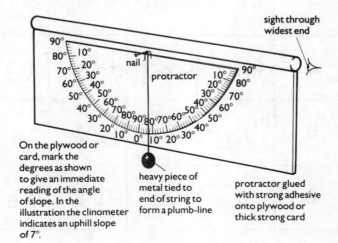

Figure 8 How to make a clinometer

- **Clinometer** – this can be made as shown in figure 8
- **Beach material measuring equipment** as on page 105. Include two extra columns in your Table for Recording Beach Material this time: 'shortest axis' and 'axis ratio'
- **Stopwatch or digital watch**

Figure 9 Scale diagram to show the differences in length between sloping ground and the horizontal

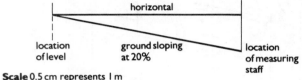

Scale 0.5 cm represents 1 m

The horizontal line measures 5 cm = 1 m
The sloping line measures 5.1 cm = 10.2 m

FIELDWORK METHOD

First lay the cord along the beach, preferably at right angles to the sea, to mark your line of transect. Weight it at both ends.

For complete accuracy the distance between sighting positions should be horizontal, but the difference between the length of sloping ground and the horizontal length is usually very small. On a slope of 20% (1 in 5) the difference for a descent of 1 m is only 2 cm, as in figure 9.

Whichever method you use, the recorder will be able to draw the profile as the work progresses. On the graph paper use 1 mm to represent 10 cm for both the horizontal and vertical measurements. It may be necessary to exaggerate the vertical scale but this can be done at home.

LEVELLING RECORDING SHEET (for method using level/clinometer)

LEVEL LOCATION	BACKSIGHT HEIGHT IN METRES	FORESIGHT HEIGHT IN METRES	DIFFERENCE IN METRES	HEIGHT ABOVE SEA LEVEL IN METRES	DISTANCE BETWEEN STAFFS IN METRES	GRADIENT	% SLOPE	COMMENTS
A	h_1 1·8	h_2 0·4	+ 1·4	1·4	d_1 14	1 in 10	10%	ridged sand
B	h_3 2·7	0	+ 2·7	4·1	d_2 7·3	1 in 2·7	37%	big pebbles
C	0	h_4 −1·6	− 1·6	2·5	d_3 8·2	1 in 5	20%	big flat pebbles

(a) Using a level or clinometer: Carry out the work as in figure 10. Decide when the angle of the slope of the beach changes and set your level to include each change as you come to it. Place your measuring staff at the change in slope.

$h_1 - h_2$ = difference in height between A and B
$h_3 - h_4$ $(h_3 - 0)$ = difference in height between B and crest
$h_5 - h_4$ $(h_5 - 0)$ = difference in height between crest and C

Always take the height recorded by the foresight from that recorded by the backsight. If the backsight reading is the smaller one, the difference is a minus quantity and this indicates that the land is sloping down. Record your results on the Levelling Recording Sheet.

If using a clinometer, measure the height above ground level of the eye of the person sighting through the clinometer and keep to the same person throughout the transect. Record your results as before.

(b) Using a bucket and tube: Look at figure 11.
Place the bucket filled with water at the first change of slope as you walk up your transect from the sea, making sure that it will not tip over and spill. Put one end of the tube into the bucket and suck the other until the tube is filled with water, making sure that all air bubbles are removed. Top up the bucket if necessary. Make sure that the tube end is higher than the bucket and hold it up vertically. Hold the tube still and the water inside it will find the same level as the water in the bucket. Use the measuring staff to measure the height of the water in the tube. Measure the distance between the bucket and the end of the tube by laying the tape measure along the beach. Record your results on a Levelling Recording Sheet similar to the one on page 112.

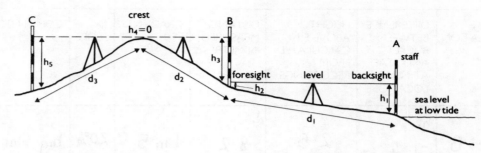

Figure 10 Levelling using a level, tripod and staff

CAUTION
As levelling is a team effort it is vital that every member of the team makes sure that he/she is doing his/her particular part of the work with the utmost accuracy. If not the results of the whole team's work will be inaccurate.

Move down the beach following the line made by the cord before you began levelling. Wherever you see a change in the angle of the slope of the beach replace the bucket there.

Measuring beach material

Follow the instructions given on page 106 and measure also the shortest axis of each pebble.

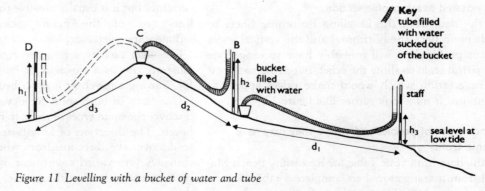

Key
tube filled with water sucked out of the bucket

Figure 11 Levelling with a bucket of water and tube

STAFF LOCATION	DIFFERENCE BETWEEN BUCKET AND STAFF AT NEXT LOCATION	HEIGHT ABOVE S.L. CALCULATED FROM RECORDINGS	DISTANCE MEASURED IN METRES	GRADIENT	% SLOPE	COMMENTS
A → B	h_1 -1·4	2·5	d_1 8·2	1 in 5	20%	big flat pebbles
B → C	h_2 2·7	4·1	d_2 7·3	1 in 2·7	37%	big flat pebbles (some spherical)
C → D	h_3 1·4	1·4	d_3 14	1 in 10	10%	ridged sand

LEVELLING RECORDING SHEET (for bucket and tube method)

PROCESSING THE INFORMATION

1 Annotated beach profile/section

Use the data from the Levelling Recording Sheet to decide upon both the horizontal and the vertical scales of your profile. You will probably have to exaggerate the vertical scale to show the relief, but avoid too great an exaggeration which would make ridges appear as mountains! It may look rather like figure 12.

2 Rock types of pebbles and where they may have come from

Use the data from your Table for Recording Beach Material from investigation 1 to complete a table like the one on page 114. The number of columns depends upon the number of different rock types in your sample. It is not always possible to name the rock type with certainty but it is usually possible to classify each pebble into one of the main **rock classes**: igneous, sedimentary, metamorphic.

Calculate each type as a percentage of the total and illustrate this as a pie-chart or bar-chart. The method for drawing a pie-chart is described on page 9.

Use maps of both solid geology and drift geology to discover the main types of rocks in the area around your beach. The direction of longshore drift may help you to discover the direction from which the material has come. A very varied assortment of the three classes of rock type suggests that the pebbles originated in glacial drift.

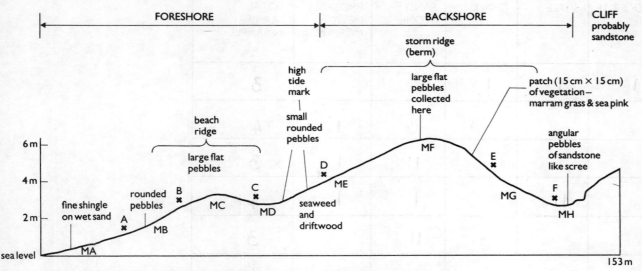

Figure 12 *Imaginary profile to show the location of beach materials*

It may be possible to map the likely origin of pebbles as a flow-line map like figure 13.

3 Calculating the axis ratio of pebbles as an index of sphericity

For each pebble, divide the longest axis by the shortest. If the number obtained is small it suggests that the pebble is almost spherical. This is only a rough measure of sphericity and to achieve a more refined result you may have time to experiment on some of the samples you brought home by using the third axis and plotting the axes on triangular graph paper. If you consider that this method produces a more accurate result you may substitute triangular graphs for the bar-charts suggested next. For each rock type collected draw a bar-chart to show the

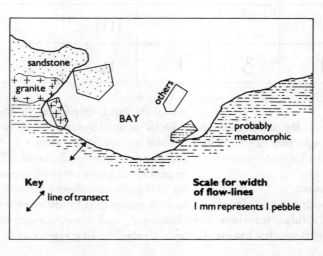

Figure 13 *Flow-line map to show where the pebbles may have come from*

LOCATION OF SAMPLE COLLECTION	GRANITE	DOLERITE	SHALE	CHALK	SAND-STONE	PROBABLY META-MORPHIC	TOTAL NUMBER IN SAMPLE
A		1	1	1			3
B	111					1	4
C					11	1	3
D			11		1	1	4
E	1				11		3
F					111	1	4
G	1				11		3
H					1111		4
TOTAL	5	1	3	1	14	4	28

axis ratio, as in figure 14.

Describe what your charts show. By reading about the mineral composition and the structure of the rocks you may be able to suggest reasons for your results.

4 Distribution of pebbles on the beach
Look again at the profile you have drawn and classify it into sections: **crest** = summit of a ridge; **foreslope** = facing the sea; **trough** = base of ridge; **backslope** =

facing the land. (See figure 15 opposite.)

Draw a scattergraph to show the distribution of pebbles on one ridge, similar to figure 6 on page 108. Plot the axis ratio on the vertical (y) axis and the weight of pebbles in grams on the horizontal (x) axis. Use a key for pebbles from different locations. You may draw separate scattergraphs for different ridges if these were very distinctive, and identify each with a name such as 'storm ridge', 'spring tide ridge'.

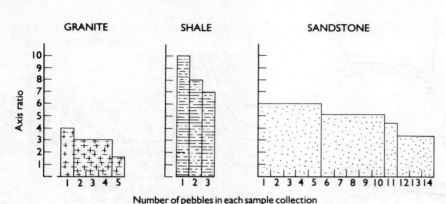

Figure 14 Bar-charts to show the shape of pebbles

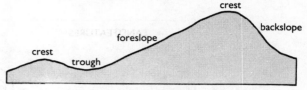

Figure 15 Profile through a storm ridge or berm

DRAWING CONCLUSIONS

1 Using the profile you have levelled and drawn, describe the distribution of materials and features upon the beach: wet sand, sand with ripples, dry sand, shingle, shells, pebbles of different shapes and sizes, rock pools, evidence of use by people.
2 Calculate the difference in height between low tide when you started your fieldwork and the most recent high tide mark. Describe any evidence you obtained to account for other tide levels.
3 Suggest reasons for the shapes of beach material which you sampled. Can you suggest where the rock types of the pebbles originated?
4 If you have investigated a pebble beach, test these hypotheses on the distribution of pebbles on a storm ridge:
   (a) 'That large flat pebbles accumulate on the crest and on the backslope, where some may be angular as a result of being thrown.'
   (b) 'That large rounded pebbles occur on the foreslope.'
   (c) 'That pebbles of all shapes and sizes are found in the trough.'

FURTHER SUGGESTION

Has your investigation led you to believe that this stretch of coastline could be developed economically: tourism, fishing, fish farming including shellfish, extraction of sand and gravel? It may be necessary to investigate the transport network and settlements in the immediate area. The chapter on 'Outdoor Leisure Area' (pages 5–19) will suggest ways of tackling the project.

3 : To investigate the ways in which people use the coast

PREPARATION

There are at least five main ways in which the coast is used: fishing, docking, leisure, industry, effluent disposal. All of these – and any others which you can think of – make use of both the shore and the adjacent land. Make lists of all the evidence for each of these that you could find along a coastline.

Look at an Ordnance Survey map of scale 1:25 000 or larger and decide upon the route along a coastline which you will follow. If you have to pass through private land, write to request permission before beginning your investigation. Trace the route from the Ordnance Survey

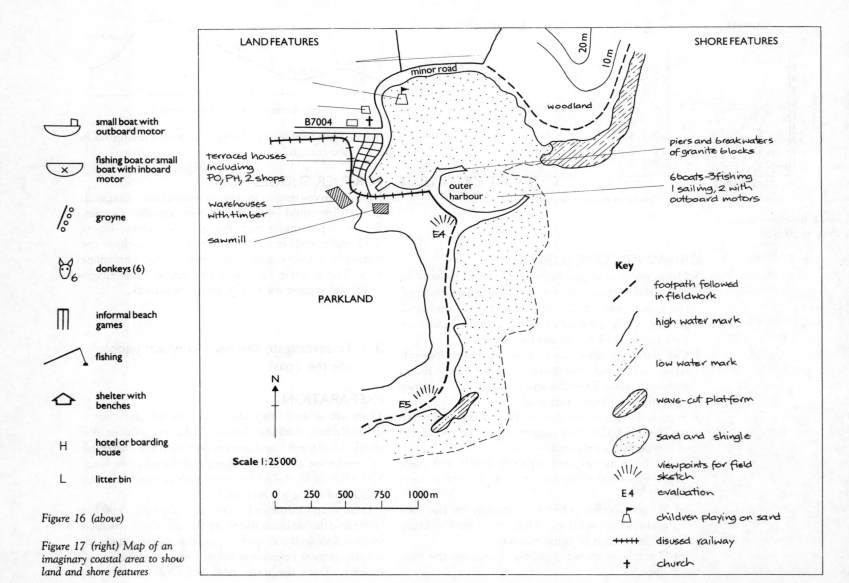

LAND FEATURES

minor road

B7004

woodland

20 m

10 m

SHORE FEATURES

piers and breakwaters of granite blocks

6 boats - 3 fishing 1 sailing, 2 with outboard motors

outer harbour

terraced houses including PO, PH, 2 shops

warehouses with timber

sawmill

E4

PARKLAND

N

E5

Scale 1:25 000

| 0 | 250 | 500 | 750 | 1000m |

Key

footpath followed in fieldwork

high water mark

low water mark

wave-cut platform

sand and shingle

viewpoints for field sketch

E4 — evaluation

children playing on sand

++++ disused railway

† church

small boat with outboard motor

fishing boat or small boat with inboard motor

groyne

donkeys (6)

informal beach games

fishing

shelter with benches

H — hotel or boarding house

L — litter bin

Figure 16 (above)

Figure 17 (right) Map of an imaginary coastal area to show land and shore features

map, enlarging it to a scale of 1:10 000 or bigger, and then mark on it buildings, field boundaries and other features.

You may decide to concentrate your investigation upon certain ways in which the coast is used, perhaps evidence of tourism or of manufacturing industry. Include on your traced map all evidence of use by people already provided on the Ordnance Survey map. Add this to the key. Consider what other features you expect to find and devise symbols for them. Figure 16 gives some examples.

Make sure that you have sufficient room on both sides of the tracing to annotate the map in the field: 'Shore features' on one side and 'Land features' on the other, as in figure 17. You will need to record features visible to a distance of 250 m from the transect and in greater detail within 25 m. Using maps of school or home and possibly a measuring tape, become familiar with these distances, so that you can estimate them by eye easily.

Practise landscape evaluation around home or school before your fieldwork. The procedure for evaluating a landscape is explained on page 11, but, of course, you will do this only at your chosen viewpoints. If you work in pairs or in a group make your evaluations in secret and compare results later. Calculate the average of your results.

It is important in your fieldwork to evaluate the impact of people's activities upon the coastline so that you can say whether or not it has spoiled the quality of the coastal landscape. Find locations on the Ordnance Survey map from which you will be able to view the landscape. The drawing of a profile will help, but take care not to exaggerate the vertical scale more than five times. Obviously the higher the point the wider your view will be, but remember to restrict your impressions to within 250 m on both sides of the coastline.

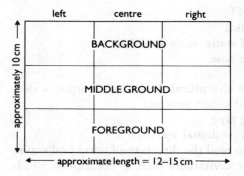

Figure 18 Framework for a field sketch

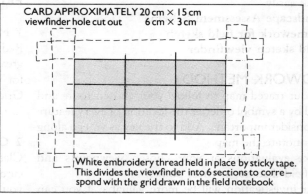

Figure 19 How to make a viewfinder for field sketching

White lines may not be sufficiently clear for you. Experiment with black or red to find the colour that suits you best.

If you make a field sketch it will help to support your evaluation. A sketch is preferable to a photograph because it enables you to emphasise the features you consider important and it can be annotated in the field. If you draw a grid in your field notebook, like the one in figure 18, it will help you to place the main features in your sketch. It is an even greater help if you make a viewfinder to match, like the one in figure 19. Hold it at arm's length and look through it with one eye.

Copy the Landscape Assessment Scheme from page 11.

EQUIPMENT
- **Basic fieldkit**
- **Tracing of route, scale 1:10 000**
- **Measuring pole,**
  or
- **Metre rule** and **plumb line** of thick string with a heavy metal weight attached
- **Measuring tape**
- **Stopwatch or digital watch**
- **Compass to read the direction of wind and waves**
- **Buckets or containers** such as biscuit tins which stack easily
- **Landscape Assessment Scheme**
- **Framework for field sketch**
- **Field sketch viewfinder**

FIELDWORK METHOD

Use your traced map to follow your chosen route and record by a symbol or letter the location of every feature you consider important. Add to the key as you go along and annotate the map.

Make evaluations at your chosen viewpoints and draw field sketches at these points.

Your investigation will be more valuable if you can find the answers to questions such as:
1. how much accommodation is available in hotels and boarding houses close to the shore;
2. why have factories been located here;
3. how many ships use the harbour each month, what tonnage are they and what draught of water do they need;
4. how long are breakwaters and when were they built?

If there are groynes on the beach, use the measuring tape to discover the distance between them, the length to which they project towards the sea and what they are made from. Use the measuring pole held vertically to find the difference between the height of material

CAUTION
Take care to keep to footpaths and roads wherever possible. Never attempt to climb cliffs or go close to the edge of the top of cliffs.

piled up on both sides. Record your measurements. What do they tell you about the usual direction from which waves approach the beach? Record the direction of wave approach on the day of your fieldwork. Why may it be different from the usual direction?

Sample the beach material at intervals along the route. Methods of investigating it are explained on pages 105–6. Collect samples to bring back. If there are changes in beach material can you suggest the reasons from observation in the field?

PROCESSING THE INFORMATION

1 Mapping the use by people
Redraw your sketch map neatly and use colours for greater clarity: yellow for sand; orange for shingle; grey for wave-cut platform; green for woodland and so on. Grid lines must be added, and these may also be drawn in colour. Add the symbols and key.

2 Calculating different types of use by people
Classify the different kinds of use, perhaps into the five categories suggested in the Preparation on page 115. If you have concentrated upon only one type of use, such as fishing or tourism, then count the number of different ways in which the coast you have investigated has been used for this purpose. Use your annotated map to count the number in each category or use. Calculate each as a percentage of the total. Illustrate your results as a bar-chart or pie-chart or if you have discovered two main categories/uses illustrate these in a Venn diagram as shown on page 5.

3 Evaluating people's impact upon the coast
Use the landscape evaluation records and your field sketches to give a numerical value of your opinion of the coastal scenery at each viewpoint. Choose a different

colour to represent each value. Make another tracing of the map of the coast and colour each section according to its attractiveness value. The shore may well be coloured differently from the land. Add a key to your map. Describe what your map shows.

DRAWING CONCLUSIONS

1 Using your maps and diagrams as illustration, describe the ways in which the coast is used by people. Suggest reasons why it is used in these ways.

2 Has your fieldwork investigation shown that good use is being made of the coast? What improvements would you suggest for any of the following:
   (a) conservation,
   (b) leisure activities,
   (c) industry,
   (d) commercial fishing?

3 Imagine that you have been asked to plan one or more tourist trails along attractive parts of the coast for people of different age-groups. Suggest the routes you would choose and the facilities you would provide for visitors, including those who come by private or public transport.

4 Imagine that you are a coastguard or a lifeguard. Suggest from your fieldwork investigation which parts of the coast you consider would have to be watched most closely. Where would you locate your headquarters? What safety precautions would you enforce?

5 Test one of these hypotheses:
   (a) 'That the natural scenery of the stretch of coastline is being badly affected by people's use.'
   (b) 'That the coast could provide more sites for manufacturing industry.'

FURTHER SUGGESTIONS

1

Assess the popularity of different stretches of the coast by carrying out investigations similar to those suggested on pages 6–10.

2

Discover the area from which visitors come to the coast. Investigate the transport network as suggested on pages 13–19. Enquire from the local Tourist Board about the amount of accommodation available along the coast and any special facilities provided, such as for conferences.

APPENDIX

All the questionnaires and lists may be produced using this computer program. It has been written for the BBC microcomputer, but could easily be adapted for use on other models.

THE PROGRAM REQUIREMENTS

User is required to input (when asked) the number of questions on the questionnaire and the maximum number of possible replies for any one question *or* part of a question.

Data is to be written from 500 onwards.

The data must be in the following order:

(i)   A number = number of parts to the question;

(ii) A number = number of possible replies to the first part of the question (if only one part, number of replies to the question);

(iii) A statement = the question (or part of the question);

(iv) Letter(s)/statement(s) = the possible replies;

If more parts to the question

(v)   A number = number of possible replies to this part.

and continue from (iii) above.

If no more parts

start question 2 etc. from (i) above.

Notes

If the reply to a question is a sentence, e.g., line 660 asks a question, then the next piece of data must be a word,

e.g., 'answer =' (this is the 'possible reply' expected in (iv) above). If more than one reply, each must be preceded by a letter 'A, B, C, D, etc.'

WEATHER QUESTIONNAIRE

1) Did it rain last week?   Yes ... No ...

2) Please tick the day or days that it rained   Sunday   ...
                                                 Monday   ...
                                                 Tuesday   ...
                                                 Wednesday   ...
                                                 Thursday   ...
                                                 Friday   ...
                                                 Saturday   ...

3) (a) During the week did the weather make
       you use or wear any special clothing?   Yes ... No ...

   (b) If the special clothing was one of the
       following tick the appropriate item :   Raincoat   ...
                                                 Rainhat   ...
                                                 Umbrella   ...
                                                 Wellingtons...
                                                 Other   ...

   (c) If the special clothing was due to dry
       weather did you leave:
       a) your coat/jacket off?   Yes ... No ...
       b) your pullover/cardigan off?   Yes ... No ...

   (d) If the special clothing was due to wet
       weather did you wear :
       Please tick the appropriate item(s) :
       a) a coat?   Yes ...
       b) a scarf?   Yes ...
       c) gloves?   Yes ...
       d) an extra pullover   Yes ...
       e) other?   Yes ...

4) Did you have any activity planned for
   Saturday or Sunday?   Yes ... No ...

   (a) Did rain affect you?   Yes ... No ...
   (b) Did heat affect you?   Yes ... No ...
   (c) Did cold affect you?   Yes ... No ...

5) Choose a day last week on which you
   remember the weather?   Sunday   ...
   Tick the day you have chosen :   Monday   ...
                                                                Tuesday   ...
                                                                Wednesday   ...
                                                                Thursday   ...
                                                                Friday   ...
                                                                Saturday   ...

   (a) Did it rain in the morning?   Yes ... No ...
       Did rain in the afternoon?   Yes ... No ...
   (b) Was it sunny in the morning?   Yes ... No ...
       Was it sunny in the afternoon?   Yes ... No ...
   (c) Was it hot?   Yes ... No ...
       Was it cold?   Yes ... No ...
   (d) Did any of the following occur?
       Tick the appropriate condition :   Hail   ...
                                                                Thunder   ...
                                                                Lightning   ...
                                                                Snow   ...
                                                                Frost   ...
                                                                Fog   ...
                                                                Mist   ...

```
10 CLS
20 PRINT "INPUT NO. OF QU.S,MAX.NO. OF PARTS TO ANY QU."
30 INPUT A,H
40 DIM Q(H),B(A,H),A$(10,10),R$(10,10,10),C$(10,10)
50 RESTORE
60 CLS
70 FOR N=1 TO A
80 READ Q(N)
90 FOR G=1 TO Q(N)
100 READ B(N,G),A$(N,G)
110 FOR X=1 TO B(N,G)
120 READ R$(N,G,X)
130 NEXT X,G,N
140 FOR N=1 TO A
150 FOR G=1 TO Q(N)
160 PRINT "QUESTION  ";N;
170 IF Q(N)>1 THEN PRINT "PART ";G
180 PRINT
190 PRINT A$(N,G)
200 FOR X=1 TO B(N,G)
210 IF B(N,G)=1 THEN PRINT R$(N,G,X) ELSE PRINT TAB(20);R$(N,G,X)
220 NEXT X
230 PRINT
240 PRINT
250 INPUT C$(N,G)
260 PRINT
270 D=ASC(C$(N,G))-64
280 IF B(N,G)=1 GOTO 350
290 IF B(N,G)>2 GOTO 340
300 IF C$(N,G)="YES" GOTO 350
310 IF C$(N,G)<>"NO" GOTO 340
320 G=G+1
330 GOTO 350
340 IF D<1 OR D>B(N,G) GOTO 250
350 NEXT G
360 NEXT N
370 CLS
380 PRINT "YOUR RESULTS ARE..."
390 PRINT
400 PRINT
```

```
410 FOR N=1 TO A
420 PRINT "QUESTION ";N;
430 FOR G=1 TO Q(N)
440 IF Q(N)>>1 THEN PRINT "PART ";G
450 PRINT
460 PRINT "...............      ";C$(N,G)
470 PRINT
480 PRINT "MAKE A COPY IF NECESSARY"
490 PRINT "PRESS RETURN TO CONTINUE"
500 INPUT J$
510 NEXT G
520 NEXT N
530 PRINT "IS THERE ANOTHER PERSON WAITING TO PUT IN THEIR RESULTS? (Y/N)"
540 INPUT P$
550 IF P$="Y" OR P$="YES" GOTO 50
560 DATA 1,2
570 DATA DID IT RAIN LAST WEEK
580 DATA YES,NO,1,7
590 DATA WHICH DAY DID IT RAIN?
600 DATA A SUN,B MON,C TUE, D WED
610 DATA E THURS,F FRI,G SAT
620 DATA 2,2
630 DATA DID RAINFALL MAKE YOU WEAR ANY SPECIAL CLOTHING?
640 DATA YES,NO
650  DATA 1
660 DATA IF YES..IN WHAT WAY?
670 DATA ANSWER
680 DATA 2,2
690 DATA DID TEMP. MAKE YOU WEAR ANY SPECIAL CLOTHING
700 DATA YES,NO
710 DATA 1
720 DATA IF YES...IN WHAT WAY?
730 DATA ANSWER
740 DATA 2,2
750 DATA DID WEATHER AFFECT WHAT YOU DID ON SAT OR SUN?
760 DATA YES,NO
770 DATA 1
780 DATA IF YES...IN WHAT WAY?
790 DATA ANSWER
800 END
```

INDEX